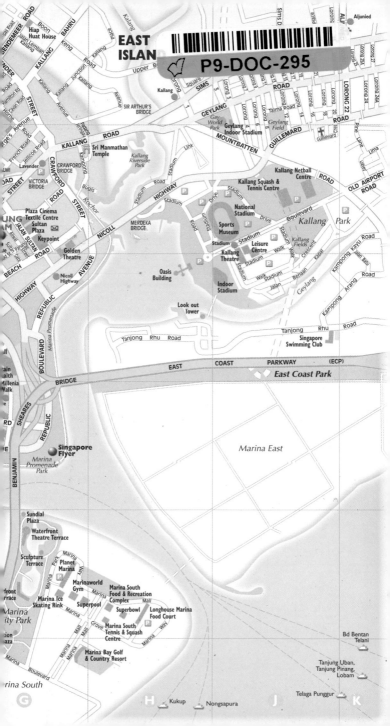

EAST ISLAN

P9-DOC-295

How to Use This Book

KEY TO SYMBOLS

✚	Map reference to the accompanying fold-out map	❓	Other practical information
✉	Address	▷	Further information
☎	Telephone number	ℹ	Tourist information
⏱	Opening/closing times	✋	Admission charges: Expensive (over S$16), Moderate (S$8–S$15), and Inexpensive (S$7 or less)
🍴	Restaurant or café		
🚆	Nearest rail station	★ Major Sight	★ Minor Sight
Ⓜ	Nearest MRT station	👣 Walks	🚌 Excursions
🚍	Nearest bus route	🏬 Shops	
⛴	Nearest riverboat or ferry stop	🎵 Entertainment and Nightlife	
♿	Facilities for visitors with disabilities	🍴 Restaurants	

This guide is divided into four sections

• Essential Singapore: An introduction to the city and tips on making the most of your stay.
• Singapore by Area: We've broken the city into four areas, and recommended the best sights, shops, entertainment venues, nightlife and restaurants in each one. Suggested walks help you to explore on foot.
• Where to Stay: The best hotels, whether you're looking for luxury, budget or something in between.
• Need to Know: The info you need to make your trip run smoothly, including getting about by public transport, weather tips, emergency phone numbers and useful websites.

Navigation In the Singapore by Area chapter, we've given each area its own tint, which is also used on the locator maps throughout the book and the map on the inside front cover.

Maps The fold-out map accompanying this book is a comprehensive street plan of central Singapore. The grid on this map is the same as the grid on The City area locator map and has upper case grid references. Sights and listings within the East Island and West Island areas have lower case grid references.

Fodor's

Singapore's
25Best

by Vivien Lytton

Fodor's Travel Publications
New York • Toronto
London • Sydney • Auckland
www.fodors.com

Contents

ESSENTIAL SINGAPORE 4–18

Introducing Singapore   4–5
A Short Stay in Singapore   6–7
Top 25   8–9
Shopping   10–11
Shopping by Theme   12
Singapore by Night   13
Eating Out   14
Restaurants by Cuisine   15
If You Like…   16–18

SINGAPORE BY AREA 19–106
THE CITY   20–52

Area Map   22–23
Sights   24–44
Walk   45
Shopping   46–47
Entertainment
  and Nightlife   48–49
Restaurants   50–52

WEST ISLAND   53–78

Area Map   54–55
Sights   56–75
Walk   76
Shopping   77
Restaurants   78

EAST ISLAND   79–92

Area Map   80–81
Sights   82–87
Walk   88
Shopping   90
Entertainment
  and Nightlife   91
Restaurants   92

FARTHER AFIELD   93–106

Area Map   94–95
Sights   96–99
Diving Singapore's
  Islands   100–101
Excursions   102–103
Walk   104
Shopping   106
Restaurants   106

WHERE TO STAY   107–112

Introduction   108
Budget Hotels   109
Mid-Range Hotels   110–111
Luxury Hotels   112

NEED TO KNOW   113–125

Planning Ahead   114–115
Getting There   116–117
Getting Around   118–119
Essential Facts   120–121
Language   122–123
Timeline   124–125

Introducing Singapore

The tiny island nation of Singapore is a dramatic fusion of the Victorian age and the 21st century. It's morphed from destitute and war-ravaged ex-colony into an affluent, educated and savvy nation—a change that's been carried out with verve and style.

Tree-lined avenues, landscaped urban areas, small parks and roadside tropical greenery are common features of this attractive, tidy city. Building on an illustrious trading history, Singapore is the world's busiest shipping port, and rivalled only by Tokyo as Asia's premier financial hub. Despite the island's impressive development, seen in the cityscape of tower blocks, freeways and glitzy malls, Singapore retains a fairly laid-back feel and pockets of the old world remain in superbly restored (or occasionally rebuilt) areas.

The diversity of race—Chinese, Malay, Indians, plus workers from other parts of Asia and the West—and their many religions, festivals and cultural practices is where Singapore sets itself apart. Ancient imported traditions remain important but a strong Singaporean identity has been forged in the country's rapid development, and relations between the races are better than many other cosmopolitan cities.

Just over 60 miles (100km) north of the equator, the island's tropical climate, with humidity often above 90 per cent, can sap the energy of most. Fortunately, air-conditioning rules in shops, hotels and public transportation facilities.

So board a bus, hop on the MRT or hail a cab and explore the delights of this vibrant island state. The neighborhoods each have a distinct character based on their ethnic or colonial origins. Visit the temples of Chinatown, the markets in Little India and the sheesh cafés in Kampung Glam and Singapore will reveal itself as much more than the shopping frenzy of Orchard Road.

Facts + Figures

- **Population in 1819: 500; population in 2006: 4.5 million**

- **Religions: Taoist/Buddhist 54%; Muslim 15%; Christian 13%; Hindu 4%; other/none 14%**

SINGLISH

You're bound to come across Singlish, the local colloquial English, if you talk to many Singaporeans. You'll know someone is speaking Singlish if they throw the word *lah* in at every opportunity to show emphasis. Other examples include: *fli-end* (friend), *tok kong* (very good) and *lerf* (love).

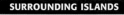

SURROUNDING ISLANDS

While the best-known island is the recreational Sentosa (▷ 62–63), once a British fort, the country is surrounded by more than 50 small islands. While they're mostly occupied by the military, oil refineries or nature reserves, St. John's Island (▷ 98) in the south is a picnic destination and Kusu Island has a turtle sanctuary.

A FINE CITY

You may have heard that Singapore is a fine city (you can even buy the T-shirt). The government's perfectly reasonable campaign to keep the city clean, and its citizens socially responsible, has led to fines of up to S$1,000 for such acts as littering, jaywalking or even failure to flush a public toilet.

A Short Stay in Singapore

DAY 1

Morning Have an early breakfast and head for the **Botanic Gardens** (▷ 56–57) for a walk among the extensive plant collection. Only a few minutes' bus ride from Orchard Road, this tropical botanical treasure-trove is at its best in the cool of the morning.

Mid-morning Take a bus or taxi back into the city and stroll along **Orchard Road** (▷ 36–37). The morning is less crowded than the afternoon and you can always come back when you've found your way around this mega shopopolis.

Lunch Make your way to **Chinatown** (▷ 28–29) for lunch, after a shower and freshen-up in your hotel. There are many authentic hawker centers here for a quintessential Singapore lunch with the locals.

Afternoon Explore Chinatown's back streets where there are many antique and gift shops—be sure to visit the **Singapore Handicraft Centre** (▷ 47). Wander down South Bridge Road to view Singapore's newest temple, the gigantic **Buddha Tooth Relic Temple** (▷ 26).

Mid-afternoon Take a bus or taxi to the **Asian Civilisations Museum** (▷ 24–25) and learn about Asian cultures from the excellent displays in this perfectly restored old colonial-period building.

Dinner Cross Cavenagh Bridge and enjoy a waterside meal at one of the seafood restaurants along Boat Quay.

Evening Head back across the river to the **Esplanade Theatres** (▷ 30) for a performance—tickets are available from the box office. Wander around the precinct and enjoy the fabulous views of the city at night.

Morning Visit **Raffles Hotel** (▷ 38) at the start of the day, a quieter time to wander around one of the world's most famous hotels, when you can enjoy a coffee instead of an expensive Singapore Sling. Check out some of the public spaces, including the famed Long Bar and visit the small museum on the second floor. Then head for the nearby **Singapore Art Museum** (▷ 39), housed in a beautifully restored 19th-century school building, which has a fine collection of Southeast Asian art.

Mid-morning Take a bus to Serangoon Road to have a look in the interesting shops that line the narrow footpaths of **Little India** (▷ 34–35).

Lunch Serangoon Road has plenty of Indian dining options, but a really economical and tasty lunch can be had at **Komala Vilas** (▷ 52).

Afternoon Take the MRT to **Harbourfront** (▷ 72) and shop away at Singapore's largest mall, **VivoCity** (▷ 47).

Mid-afternoon Catch the MRT from Harbourfront to **Clarke Quay** (▷ 27) via Chinatown. Explore the shops around Clarke Quay and perhaps take a boat ride on the Singapore River.

Dinner The riverside setting of **Clarke Quay** (▷ 27), illuminated by the city lights, makes a perfect evening meal destination. Expatriates congregate here after a hard day at the office for drinks and to dine. There are any number of fine dining options along the river.

Evening There are some good nightspots here, but try the largest Asian edition of the UK's Ministry of Sound for dancing. **The Pump Room** (▷ 49) is a slightly more chilled out, but no less hip, alternative.

Top 25

► ► ►

Asian Civilisations Museum ▷ 24–25 Asian history and culture in two stunning buildings.

Botanic Gardens ▷ 56–57 Superbly landscaped gardens full of tropical and subtropical flora.

Buddha Tooth Relic Temple ▷ 26 An enormous Buddhist haven in the heart of the city.

Singapore Zoo ▷ 70–71 Often hailed as one of the loveliest zoos in the world.

Singapore Science Centre ▷ 68–69 The Science Centre introduces children to science and technology in an entertaining hands-on style.

Singapore Nature Reserves ▷ 66–67 Escape the city to tropical open spaces.

Singapore Flyer ▷ 40 There are spectacular views across Singapore from the world's largest observation wheel.

Singapore Discovery Centre ▷ 64 A fascinating, world-class "edutainment" attraction.

Singapore Art Museum ▷ 39 Local and Asian art is beautifully displayed at this state-of-the-art gallery.

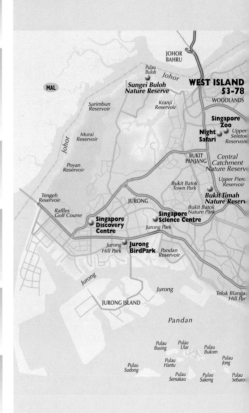

Sentosa ▷ 62–63 An island playground with a fabulous cable-car ride.

Raffles Hotel and Museum ▷ 38 One of the world's greatest palace-hotels.

Pulau Ubin ▷ 96–97 An offshore island idyll offering a chance to get away from it all.

8

These pages are a quick guide to the Top 25, which are described in more detail later. Here they are listed alphabetically, and the tinted background shows which area they are in.

Changi Chapel & Museum ▷ **82** A moving record of conditions endured by prisoners held during WWII.

Chinatown ▷ **28–29** Conveys something of the flavor of old Singapore.

Clarke Quay ▷ **27** The renovated quayside has become a popular night-time venue.

East Coast Park ▷ **84–85** Singaporeans head to this beachside area for land and sea sports or to just chill.

Esplanade–Theatres on the Bay ▷ **30** A fantastic world-class theater and entertainment complex.

Joo Chiat Road ▷ **83** The traditional Singapore way of life can still be seen in this nostalgic area.

Jurong BirdPark ▷ **58–59** Home to more than 9,000 birds from all over the world.

Kampung Glam ▷ **31** Historic district named after the glam tree.

Lau Pa Sat ▷ **32** Food stalls line a Victorian cast-iron building

Little India ▷ **34–35** The exotic sights, sounds and smells of southern India.

Orchard Road ▷ **36–37** A tree-lined boulevard offering some of Singapore's best shopping.

Night Safari ▷ **60–61** Take the tram ride around this park and see creatures in their night-time habitats.

National Museum of Singapore ▷ **33** Singapore's history comes to life here.

ESSENTIAL SINGAPORE TOP 25

Shopping

Shopping in Singapore is a very serious activity. Without a doubt, the city is Southeast Asia's shopping capital and shops seem to outnumber its inhabitants.

Singapore's Orchard Road (▷ 36–37) provides a comprehensive shopping experience equal to other world capitals, and is particularly recommended for brand-name fashion goods, electronics and cameras. But the benefit of Singapore shopping to those interested in ethnic arts and crafts or Asian antiques is that the nation state's racial mix of Chinese, Malay and Indian means that all types of goods from these cultures can be found in the specialist shops, especially those in the different ethnic quarters of the city. From the Chinese area you will find porcelain, masks, silk and traditional paintings; from the Malay there's basketware, lkat cloth, batiks, puppets, sarongs and leatherware; and from the Indian quarter paintings, jewelry, sculptures and pottery.

Not surprisingly, given Singapore's hot and humid weather, every large building has air-conditioning. Major Orchard Road department stores include Tangs, Robinsons and Takashimaya. Be sure to check out Far East Plaza in Scotts Road for younger fashions. For small, inexpensive souvenirs, take the MRT to Bugis. For cameras and electronic equipment try Lucky Plaza and Sim Lim Square, armed with your STB good retailers guide (▷ 11) and the Funan Digitalife Mall on North Bridge Road. The huge Marina Square, including Millenia Walk,

DUTY-FREE LAWS

Singapore's Tourist Refund Scheme means you can claim back 7 per cent Goods and Services Tax on large purchases when you depart from Chaingi Airport. Whenever you spend more than S$100 with a single retailer in a single day, ask for a copy of the GST tax refund form and present it to airport customs officials to claim your refund.

Singapore's shopping is some of the best in the world—particularly along the famous Orchard Road

five minutes' walk from Raffles City MRT station, has lots of homeware shops. Chinatown has a mix of souvenir and antiques shops, including the very interesting People's Park Complex—still popular with locals—a good example of Singapore retailing circa the 1960s. In the colonial district try the lovely CHIJMES mall and nearby Raffles City for fashion and food. Antiques lovers should check out Tanglin Mall and the Paragon Shopping Centre. For an Indian department store experience, try the Mustafa Centre in Serangoon Road which opens 24 hours, every day of the year. While bargaining in the markets and suburban shops is considered part of the Singapore experience, and most electronic stores and jewelers will allow you to haggle a little, brand-name boutiques and department stores throughout Singapore have fixed and clearly marked prices.

As you would expect, retailing is evolving in Singapore. Shopping has become such a lifestyle activity that new destinations such as VivoCity meld entertainment with shopping in architectually stimulating surroundings. The Sunday flea market at the China Square Central Mall (Cross Street) is a little less polished, but for real old Singaporean charm head to the outdoor Thieves Market on Sungei Road. It's particularly festive after dark.

CONSUMER PROTECTION

Since Singaporeans and the 6 million annual visitors to the island take shopping seriously, the Singapore government is very keen to promote hassle-free, safe shopping for consumers. To aid and protect shoppers, the STB (Singapore Tourism Board) publishes a shopping guide (available at tourism offices) which lists good retailers—those preferred retailers chosen for their service and reliability—and a list of retailers to avoid. A special hotline number, 1800 736 2000, has been set up to assist tourists who have had bad retail experiences during their stay in Singapore. You can also email feedback@stb.com.sg.

Shopping by Theme

Whether you're looking for a department store, a quirky boutique, or something in between, you'll find it all in Singapore. On this page shops are listed by theme. For a more detailed write-up, see the individual listings in Singapore by Area.

ANTIQUES AND HANDICRAFTS

Antiques of the Orient (▷ 77)
Burmese Fine Arts (▷ 77)
Lim's Arts & Crafts (▷ 77)
Mata Hari Antiques (▷ 77)
Singapore Handicraft Centre (▷ 47)

BOOKS

Books Kinokuniya (▷ 37)
Select Books (▷ 77)

DEPARTMENT STORES

Mustafa Centre (▷ 46)
Takashimaya (▷ 37)
Tangs (▷ 47)
Yue Hwa Chinese Products Emporium (▷ 47)

EASTERN TRADING GOODS

Batik Emporium (▷ 90)
Holland Road Shopping Centre (▷ 77)

Poppy Fabric (▷ 90)
Thandapani Co (▷ 90)

ELECTRICAL AND ELECTRONIC GOODS

Apple Centre at Funan (▷ 46)
Cathay Photo Store (▷ 46)
Funan Digitalife Mall (▷ 46)
Sim Lim Square (▷ 90)

SHOPPING MALLS AND STREETS

Arab Street (▷ 41)
Bintan Mall (▷ 106)
Bugis Junction (▷ 90)
Bugis Street (▷ 41)
Centrepoint (▷ 46)
Chinatown Point (▷ 49)
Changi Village (▷ 90)
Clarke Quay (▷ 29)
Geylang Serai (▷ 90)
The Heeren (▷ 46)
Johor Bahru Duty Free Complex (Zon) (▷ 106)
Lucky Plaza (▷ 46)

Millenia Walk (▷ 46)
Ngee Ann City (▷ 37)
Orchard Road (▷ 36–37)
People's Park Complex (▷ 46)
Plaza Pelangi (▷ 106)
Raffles City (▷ 47)
Suntec City Mall (▷ 47)
Tanglin Mall (▷ 77)
Tanglin Shopping Centre (▷ 77)
Temple/Pagoda/Trengganu Streets (▷ 47)
Thieves Market (▷ 47)
VivoCity (▷ 47)

WATCHES AND JEWELRY

Apollo Goldsmiths (▷ 90)
Pidemco Centre (▷ 47)
Terese Jade & Minerals (▷ 77)

Singapore by Night

Singapore is one of the world's great night cities, whether you want to shop, party or go on a safari.

Stepping Out

Retail stores remain open until 9 or 10pm daily (late shopping until 11pm every Saturday on Orchard Road), hawker food stands and restaurants provide fantastic choices of cuisine, and bars and clubs are often still packed into the early hours. Main areas to head for include Orchard Road (especially Emerald Hill); Boat, Robertson and Clarke quays; Chinatown (Far East Square district); and the Colonial District (CHIJMES). Around Bugis Street there's always some action, although the area is not as risqué as it was when it was the transsexual meeting place. Expats frequent Holland Village or the Orchard Road hotels.

Riverside Action

Arguably the best choice for those new to town is to head for Boat Quay or Clarke Quay (▷ 27) districts. Both areas have walkways, bars, clubs and restaurants to choose from, and a riverside nightlife ambience that is typically Singaporean. Alternatively, take an evening river cruise to get a different perspective of the city, with its old and new architecture and the night lights. Or head for one of the nightspots (▷ 48–49) for live or house music and a chance to party with the locals.

Fun Round the Clock

There is a glut of after-dark attractions in the city. It is now possible to go on a safari, play golf and make a bungee jump long after dusk.

There's plenty to do in Singapore at night. It's a safe city, too

DRINKING OUT

To get the night off to a good start, and to compensate for Singapore's noticeably high drink prices, take advantage of the happy hours that run from around 5pm until 8pm. Also, many places offer cheap or free drinks for women—check with bars and clubs beforehand (▷ 48–49).

Eating Out

From such a vibrant and polyglot society you would expect an equally diverse range of food and restaurant choices, and Singapore does not disappoint.

Whether you want to eat a spicy dish wrapped in a banana leaf in a crowded, noisy food hall, or sit down in air-conditioned grandeur and dine on haute cuisine to the tinkling of a baby grand, Singapore offers you both choices and everything in between.

Culinary choices come from Malaysia, China, India and Indonesia, and "Singapore food" is a blend of all of these. Cantonese and Fijian cooking is prevalent, but so are the lesser-known food choices from Southern China, either hawked in the street at steaming food stalls where the occupants talk at rapid-fire speed, or in tiny Chinese restaurants tucked away in Chinatown's back alleys.

Indian food is known the world over, but here you can try Malay Muslim or Indian Muslim fare. Known as "Mamak" food, you will know where to go to get this by looking for the restaurant signs written in Arabic.

For coffee, by all means head for Starbucks, but Singapore's traditional coffee shops are no-nonsense, cheap and cheerful options for popular rice and noodle dishes, along with coffee that is thick and sweet.

Local cuisine is a fusion of Malaysian, Chinese, Indian and Indonesian

---

HAND OR CUTLERY?

Many Hindus and Muslims eat their food with the right hand only; it is considered unclean to eat with the left hand, although it's okay to use utensils—usually a fork and spoon. Eating with your hand, you tear pieces of chapati (using only one hand) and then soak or scoop up elements of the meal. For rice there's another technique: you add the curries and work up the mixture into balls, which you then pick up and pop—almost flick—into your mouth.

Restaurants by Cuisine

There are restaurants to suit all tastes and budgets in Singapore. On this page they are listed by cuisine. For a more detailed description of each restaurant, see Singapore by Area.

CHINESE

Beng Thin Hoon Kee (▷ 51)
Blue Ginger (▷ 51)
Crystal Jade (▷ 51)
Imperial Herbal Restaurant (▷ 92)
Lei Garden (▷ 92)
New Hong Kong Restaurant (▷ 106)
Wak Lok Cantonese Restaurant (▷ 92)

COFFEE AND TEA

The Chocolate Factory (▷ 51)
Coffee Club, Holland Village (▷ 78)
Raffles Hotel (▷ 38)

HAWKER CENTERS

China Square (▷ 51)
Chinatown Food Street (▷ 29)
East Coast Lagoon Food Centre (▷ 92)
Lau Pa Sat (▷ 32)
Maxwell Road Food Centre (▷ 28)
Taman Sri Tebrau Hawker Centre (▷ 106)

INDIAN

Banana Leaf Apollo (▷ 92)
Komala Vilas (▷ 52)
Mango Tree (▷ 92)
Rang Mahal (▷ 52)
Samy's Curry (▷ 78)

ITALIAN

Al Forno Trattoria (▷ 78)
La Forketta (▷ 78)
Michelangelo's (▷ 78)
Pasta Brava (▷ 52)
Pete's Place (▷ 52)
Prego (▷ 52)
Rocky's (▷ 78)
Sketches Pasta & Wine Bar (▷ 92)
Zambucca (▷ 52)

OTHER ASIAN FARE

Colours by the Bay (▷ 92)
Hae Bok's Korean Restaurant (▷ 51)
Indochine (▷ 51)

OTHER WESTERN FARE

China Square (▷ 51)
Paulaner Bräuhaus (▷ 52)
Restaurant Ember (▷ 52)
Rochester Park (▷ 78)

SEAFOOD

Chin Wah Heng Seafood (▷ 92)
Jumbo Seafood (▷ 92)
Season 'Live' Seafood (▷ 106)

VEGETARIAN

Komala Vilas (▷ 52)
Original Sin (▷ 78)
Sri Vijaya (▷ 52)
Supernature (▷ 52)

If You Like...

However you'd like to spend your time in Singapore, these top suggestions should help you tailor your ideal visit. Each sight or listing has a fuller write-up elsewhere in the book.

SAMPLING LOCAL CUISINE

Sample delicious Asian cuisines at Lau Pa Sat hawker centre (▷ 32), in the business district, where you'll find a wide variety of Asian cuisines at super-low prices.
Indian food that is inexpensive and tasty, and eaten from a banana leaf, can be found at Komala Vilas (▷ 52), in Little India.

OUTDOOR DINING

Head south of Orchard Road to the Singapore River, where Clarke Quay (▷ 27) has many riverside restaurants and bars.
Seafood lovers should head for Jumbo Seafood (▷ 92). There, waterside walking trails will help you lose the pounds you put on over lunch.

Lau Pa Sat (top); crabs at Clarke Quay (above); Orchard Road street sign (below)

ELECTRONIC GOODS

Go to Lucky Plaza (▷ 46), in Orchard Road, to check out several levels of shops selling cameras, iPods and other electricals.
For price comparisons and plenty of stores offering the latest gizmos and electronic wizardry at (almost) fixed prices, head for the Funan Digitalife Mall (▷ 46).

BRAND-NAME CLOTHES

Start at upmarket Tangs (▷ 47) and Takashimaya (▷ 37), two of Singapore's top department stores.
The huge Ngee Ann City (▷ 37) has eight levels of retail glory.

Designer shop on Orchard Road (right)

LEARNING ABOUT LOCAL CULTURE

Start at the National Museum of Singapore (▷ 33) then visit the nearby Asian Civilisations Museum (▷ 24–25) and the Singapore Art Museum (▷ 39).

Little India (▷ 34–35) is living culture, so wander around the main streets and back alleys and watch the locals go about their daily chores.

GOING OUT ON THE TOWN

Clarke Quay (▷ 27) offers a wide range of drinking, dining and nightclub options. Come here and join the expats in a beer.

Ready to kick back and dance the night away? Then head for Zouk (▷ 49), Singapore's most famous nightclub.

Singapore Art Museum (top); Clarke Quay (above); Little India (below)

STAYING AT BUDGET HOTELS

The holy grail in this pricey hotel city is good, clean accommodation that won't break the bank. YMCA International House (▷ 109), in Orchard Road, is an old favorite.

Little India Guest House (▷ 109), slap bang in the hustle and bustle of Little India, offers basic facilities.

ENTERTAINING THE KIDS

Sentosa (▷ 62–63) will entertain the young ones for a day or more, with its cable-car ride, beaches and aquarium.

The Singapore Science Centre (▷ 68–69) has heaps of hands-on interactive exhibits and lots of color and scientific movement.

Singapore Science Centre Human Anatomy section (left)

Singapore night lights (below); Bukit Timah (middle)

A POSH NIGHT OUT

The stylish cocktail Post Bar at the Fullerton Hotel (▷ 49) serves a wide selection of classic cocktails in elegant surroundings.
The highest publicly accessible point in Singapore, the Swisshotel's 72nd story New Asia Bar (▷ 49) is an essential big-night warm-up.

A WALK ON THE WILD SIDE

Start early or late to avoid the midday heat for a walk along the trails of Bukit Timah (▷ 66), a patch of primary tropical rainforest within reach of the city center.
Singapore's only protected wetland, the 130ha (321-acre) Sungei Buloh Wetland Reserve (▷ 67), is home to over 500 species of tropical flora and fauna.

THRILL SEEKING

A new pair of adrenaline attractions at Clarke Quay (▷ 27) are the G Max Reverse Bungee and the GX5, which allows five riders to freefall and swing out across the Singapore River.
Buzz down the 650m (708 yards) Sentosa Luge track—at night. This part go-kart, part toboggan run is open to 9.30pm daily (▷ 62–63).

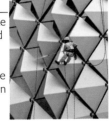

BIRDS AND ANIMALS

Esplanade concert hall roof (above); ostrich at Jurong BirdPark (below)

One of the world's best places to view tropical birds is at Jurong BirdPark (▷ 58–59), where over 8,000 species are kept in aviaries and walk-through enclosures.
Seeing nocturnal animals at a time when they are active is made easy and informative by a ride on the tram at the Night Safari (▷ 60–61).

Singapore by Area

Sights 24–44

Walk 45

Shopping 46–47

Entertainment
and Nightlife 48–49

Restaurants 50–52

THE CITY

Sights 56–75

Walk 76

Shopping 77

Restaurants 78

WEST ISLAND

Sights 82–87

Walk 88

Shopping 90

Entertainment
and Nightlife 91

Restaurants 92

EAST ISLAND

Sights 96–99

Diving Singapore's
Islands 100–101

Excursions 102–103

Walk 104

Shopping 106

Restaurants 106

FARTHER AFIELD

The City

Immerse yourself in the galleries of world-class museums, stroll the vibrant streets and back lanes of Chinatown, or take a walk down Orchard Road.

Sights	24–44
Walk	45
Shopping	46–47
Entertainment and Nightlife	48–49
Restaurants	50–52

Top 25

Asian Civilisations Museum ▷ **24**
Buddha Tooth Relic Temple ▷ **26**
Chinatown ▷ **28**
Esplanade–Theatres on the Bay ▷ **30**
Kampung Glam ▷ **31**
La Pau Sat ▷ **32**
National Museum of Singapore ▷ **33**
Little India ▷ **34**
Orchard Road ▷ **36**
Raffles Hotel and Museum ▷ **38**
Singapore Art Museum ▷ **39**
Singapore Flyer ▷ **40**

BALESTIER ROAD

RANGOON ROAD

Kallang

Sri V Temple

Sakaya Muni Buddha Gaya Temple

Sri Sivan Temple

LAVENDER STREET

KALLANG BAHRU

Farrer Park

Sri Srinivasa Perumal Temple

Serangoon Plaza

New World Park

Jln Besar Stadium

KALLANG ROAD

Angullia Mosque

SYED

Museum of Shanghai Toys

ALWI

KALLANG ROAD

Sri Manmathan Temple

INDIA

SERANGOON

JALAN

ROCHOR

SYED ALWI BRIDGE

CRAWFORD

Lavender

CRAWFORD BRIDGE

Bugis

Kallang Riverside Park

VICTORIA BRIDGE

Sim Lim Square

Abdul Gaffoor Mosque

Muslim Cemetery

CANAL

Old Malay Cemetery

VICTORIA

JALAN SULTAN

Plaza Cinema Textile Centre

KAMPUNG GLAM

Sultan Plaza

ROCHOR

OPHIR

Rochor Centre

Sultan Mosque

SULTAN ROAD

Keypoint

NICOLL

HIGHWAY

MERDEKA BRIDGE

Arab Street

NORTH BRIDGE

BEACH

Golden Theatre

Nicoll Highway

AVENUE

Bugis Junction

Bugis

Parkview Square

Bugis Street

DHL Balloon

ROAD

REPUBLIC

Marina Promenade

St Joseph's Church

St Peter & Paul

National Library

VICTORIA

MINT Museum of Toys

NICOLL

BEACH

Suntec City Mall

BOULEVARD

Bras Basah

Singapore International Convention and Exhibition Centre

Fountain of Wealth

BRIDGE

Raffles City

Raffles Hotel and Museum

Millenia Walk

REPUBLIC

St Andrew's Cathedral

Esplanade

Promenade

City Hall

War Memorial Park

RAFFLES BOULEVARD

Kim Seng Fountain

Marina Square

Wangz Biz Centre

Singapore Flyer

CONNAUGHT

RAFFLES

Cenotaph

RAFFLES AVENUE

SHERRES

BENJAMIN

Padang

DRIVE

Esplanade Theatres on the Bay

Marina Promenade Park

Victoria Concert Hall & Theatre

Lim Bo Seng Memorial

Outdoor Theatre

The Edge

Asian Civilisations Museum

ESPLANADE BRIDGE

Merlion Park

Raffles Place

Clifford Pier

Marina Bay

QUAY

One Raffles Quay

COLLYER

MARINA STATION ROAD

Bd Bentan Telani, Lobam, Tanjung Uban, Tanjung Pinang, Telaga Punggur,

The City

F   G   H

Asian Civilisations Museum

HIGHLIGHTS

- Chinese history timeline
- Red bat motifs
- Buddhist statues
- Literati gallery
- Jade collection
- Qing Dynasty porcelain
- Kang tables
- Islamic collection

TIP

- Guided tours, given several times a day, are the perfect way to learn more about Asian culture.

Displaying relics of mainland China, continental India, Islamic West Asia and Southeast Asian cultures, this excellent museum is housed in a gorgeous colonial waterfront building.

Scene setter The imposing 1865 Empress Place building sets the stage for a fascinating look at the artistic, cultural and religious developments of Asia. The continent has been cleverly divided into four distinct regions—China, Southeast Asia, West Asia (the Islamic world) and the Indian subcontinent. Like the National Museum of Singapore (▷ 33) and the prestigious Singapore Art Museum (▷ 39), this museum is managed by Singapore's National Heritage Board. Special exhibitions further explore the cultures of these parts of the world.

Clockwise from left: a sandstone figure of Buddha (Cambodia, 11th–12th century); a Chinese porcelain Buddha; the museum exterior; a Kraak dish showing two Persian ladies of the Safavid period; Lakhoun Khaol dance mask from Cambodia and a gamelan display

Multimedia There are a total of 11 theme galleries spread over three levels, displaying over 1,300 artifacts that represent a microcosm of Asian civilizations.

The story of Asia is showcased with displays, interactive exhibits and multimedia presentations to help you learn more about the multifaceted aspects of Asian cultures.

The Singapore River Gallery tells many stories, of Chinese "coolies," indigenous Orang Laut from Malaya and the more recently arrived Europeans. The West Asia Gallery has explanations of the importance of the mosque in Islamic societies. The Southeast Asia Gallery is full of lavish textile exhibits, while the China Gallery has a fascinating "interview with the Emperor" video display, and a stunning life-size example of the Son of Heaven's yellow ceremonial robe.

THE BASICS

www.acm.org.sg
⊞ F6
✉ 1 Empress Place
☎ 6332 7798
🕐 Mon 1–7, Tue–Sun 9–7, (Fri until 9)
🍴 Indochine Waterfront Restaurant; bar; café
🚇 Raffles Place
🚌 75, 100, 130, 131, 167
♿ Good
💲 Moderate
❓ Free guided tours Mon 2, Tue–Fri 11, 2; Sat, Sun 11, 2, 3, 4. Museum shops. Temporary exhibitions

Buddha Tooth Relic Temple

The temple (left); a Buddha on display (right)

THE BASICS

www.btrts.org.sg

➕ E7

✉ 288 South Bridge Road

☎ 6220 0220

🕐 Daily 7–7

🍴 Chinatown Food Street is on Smith Street, just north of the temple.

🚇 Chinatown MRT, 5 min

♿ Good to first four levels, though stairs lead to roof garden

🎟 Free

HIGHLIGHTS

● Dharma Hall
● Buddha Tooth Relic Stupa
● The Buddhist Culture Museum
● Huge reliquary from Tibet
● 10,000 Buddha Temple

TIP

● It's possible to get great pictures of the Dharma Hall from the easy-to-miss mezzanine, which rings the circumference of the hall.

The newest addition to the temples along South Bridge Street is the biggest and best yet. To a parade that already marks Christianity, Hinduism and Islam, Buddhism has burst onto the scene.

Several floors This imperious new building, opened in 2007, was designed as a mixture of Tang-dynasty palace and traditional Buddhist mandala—a spiral structure representing a Buddhist's ascent toward nirvana. There are four levels, but the building is around seven stories high thanks to a rooftop garden and a ground floor Dharma Hall, where prayer ceremonies can take place.

Highlights On the second floor an exhibition hall contains religious objects as well as a Depository of Buddhist Texts. Arguably the highlight of the temple is the third-floor Buddhist Culture Museum with a fantastic display of Buddhist items from across South East Asia and the subcontinent. Don't miss the relics chamber with ornate reliquaries, receptacles for storing body parts of Buddhism's most senior figures. The fourth floor houses the Buddha Tooth Relic inside a golden stupa, and provides a quiet place for meditation. The rooftop garden contains the 10,000 Buddha Temple, which houses a giant prayer wheel.

Education Unlike the other places of worship nearby, the temple encourages non-Buddhists to enter the most sacred parts of the temple and goes out of its way to provide good explanations of the basic tenets of Buddhism.

Riverside Point shopping mall (left); chefs preparing food in one of Clarke Quay's many restaurants (right)

Clarke Quay

Like Singapore's food options, the range of nightlife venues has grown so large that it's difficult to pick the best. But, for its scenic—and central—location, the renovated Clarke Quay is tough to beat.

Working quay Just upriver from the marina and the Raffles landing site, Clarke Quay was at the heart of the 19th trade route through Singapore. As recently as the 1980s, this riverside strand was a hive of frenetic maritime entrepreneurialism.

Revival These days the whole quay area is owned by one of Asia's biggest real estate companies who have given it a multimillion-dollar facelift that fully opened in summer 2007. Five art deco godowns (blocks of warehouses) have been refurbished in pastel hues, but the historic grandeur has been given a modern finish thanks to a climate-control canopy. Smaller lampshade covers line the riverfront and make it possible to sit out by the water without being bothered by the heat. In total, there are 62 eating, entertainment, drinking, retail and lifestyle outlets, including some essential night stops: The Arena (live music), Pump Room (bar) and Ministry of Sound (club). It's a must-visit for tourists, but part of the attraction is that it's a party spot also loved by locals.

Thrill rides The latest addition to Clarke Quay is a pair of adrenaline rides—the Reverse Bungee and G-Max. The former pings riders skyward at speed, the other is a giant swing that arcs out across the Singapore River.

THE BASICS

www.clarkequay.com.sg
- E6
- 3 River Valley Road
- 6337 3292
- 24 hours
- Various
- Clarke Quay MRT
- Generally good
- Individual venues may charge a cover

HIGHLIGHTS

- Reverse Bungee and G-Max
- Ministry of Sound
- Indochine restaurant

TIP

- Come prepared for lots of walking as you'll be tempted to check out interesting backstreets.

THE CITY ★ **TOP 25**

27

Chinatown

HIGHLIGHTS

● Maxwell Road Food Centre
● Ann Siang Hill
● Chinese shophouses
● Chinese lanterns
● Chinese museum

TIP

● Come prepared for lots of walking as you'll be tempted to check out interesting back-streets.

The best time to visit is just before Chinese New Year, when the streets throb and vibrant stands sell everything from waxed ducks to *hong bao*, red packets for giving money as presents.

Singapore's Chinatown This area covers the streets leading off South Bridge Road between Maxwell Road and the Singapore River. As a policy, conservation of the old buildings goes hand-in-hand with new development here, and though an improvement over destruction, the often rather cosmetic results and years of unsympathetic infilling have left only a few streets with the authentic atmosphere and activities of old Chinatown.

What to see Erskine Road and Ann Siang Hill exhibit some of the best efforts of preservation.

Clockwise from left: detail from Thin Hock Keng Temple; outside Thain Hock Keng Temple; aerial view of Chinatown; umbrellas for sale; shop façades and Maxwell Road hawker center

Temple and Trengganu streets have many traditional shophouses and coffee shops. While Pagoda Street, similar in character, also has the Chinatown Heritage Centre. Nearby Smith Street is the area's appointed 'food alley' with lots of covered outdoor eating options. People's Park Complex, on Eu Tong Sen Street, offers a wide range of goods, including Chinese herbs and good jewelry. South Bridge Road, between Upper Cross Street and Maxwell Road, is home to fascinating places of worship. Telok Ayer Street, although much renovated, is also worth a visit. Thian Hock Keng Temple (the Temple of Heavenly Happiness) is the oldest Chinese temple in the city. The original temple was built in 1840 by Hokkien immigrants. Far East Square includes Fuk Tak Ch'i, a former temple that now houses a museum dedicated to Singapore's Chinese immigrants.

THE BASICS

✚ E7

✉ South Bridge Road and surrounding streets

🍴 Smith Street

🚇 Chinatown

🚌 2, 5, 12, 33, 51, 61, 62, 63, 81, 84, 103, 104, 124, 143, 145, 147, 166, 174, 181, 190, 197, 520, 851

♿ None

💷 Free

Esplanade—Theatres on the Bay

Esplanade Theatres on the Bay by night (left) and by day (right)

THE BASICS

www.esplanade.com

⊞ F6

✉ 1 Esplanade Drive

☎ 6828 8377

🕐 Daily 10–10

🍴 Cafés, restaurants

🚇 City Hall

♿ Good

✋ Free entry; tours moderate

❓ Guided tours (45 min) in English Mon–Fri 11, 2, Sat, Sun 11. Tours also allow you to explore by yourself by renting a PDA loaded with information about the center

HIGHLIGHTS

- Twin glass domes
- Waterfront vistas
- High-quality performances
- Stunning concert hall
- Free performances
- Excellent restaurants
- Esplanade Mall shopping

Singapore's stunning waterfront theater and entertainment complex, dubbed the Durians for its two prickly domes, represents the government's attempt to attract world-class performers to Singapore.

Cutting-edge architecture The S$600-million Esplanade is a bid for regional arts excellence. The architect's challenge, given the tropical climate and the desire to present patrons with a dramatic view of the surroundings, was to design an essentially glazed building that was protected from the sun and heat. The fixed exterior triangular aluminum sun shields, set to be opened or closed depending on the angle of the sun, were the final design solution.

World-class facilities The Esplanade includes the Concert Hall, with 1,600 seats and a 200-seat choir stall; the Lyric Theatre, seating 2,000, modeled on a traditional Italian opera house with one stall and three tiers; and a smaller theater for drama, dance and recital, with 750 seats. Internal venues were designed to accommodate the louder and more percussive styles of Asian performances, although the flexible acoustics also suit Western orchestras.

Shopping and dining Esplanade Mall, on three levels, offers a diverse retail mix, from fashion to flowers, home decorations to handmade pottery, and there are several premier restaurants and specialty cafés and bars.

Sultan Mosque (left); at prayer in the mosque (middle) and pashminas on sale (right)

Kampung Glam

The impressive golden domes and minarets of Sultan Mosque, glinting in the late-afternoon sun, and the call of the muezzin, remind you that this area of Singapore is very much part of the Islamic world.

In the past Kampung Glam, where the Sultan of Singapore lived, was set aside in the early days for Malay, Arab and Bugis (Sulawesi) traders. The "Glam" may be named after the *gelam* tree from which medicinal oil was produced.

Today Although there are 80 mosques on the island, Sultan Mosque is the focus of worship for Singapore's Muslim (mainly Malay) community. There has been a mosque on this site since 1824, when the East India Company made a grant for its construction. The present mosque dates from 1928, and reveals an interesting mix of Middle Eastern and Moorish influences. Its gilded dome is impressive; unusually, its base is made from bottles. Seen as you walk up Bussorah Street, with its shophouses at the rear, the mosque is truly stunning. Visitors are welcome outside prayer times, as long as they are well covered—no shorts. The *istana* (palace), built in the 1840s, is at the top of Sultan Gate and houses the Malay Heritage Centre. The surrounding streets are good sources for *souk* items like basketware, perfume, batik and leather goods. The nearby Muslim coffee shops serve a wide range of Indian Muslim dishes, such as *murtabak* (pancake with various fillings) and *mee goreng* (spicy fried noodles).

THE BASICS

Sultan Mosque
➕ G4
✉ 3 Muscat Street
☎ 6293 4405
🕐 Daily 11–7
🍴 Numerous coffee shops
🚇 Bugis
🚌 2, 32, 51, 61, 63, 84, 133, 145, 197
♿ None
💳 Free

HIGHLIGHTS

● Bussorah Street
● Gilded dome of Sultan Mosque
● Prayer hall
● Istana Kampung Glam
● Murtabak
● Batik
● Haji Lane
● Malay Heritage Centre

Lau Pa Sat

The entrance to the market (left); the magnificent interior (right)

HIGHLIGHTS

- Boon Tat Street
- Hainan Chicken Rice
- Laksa
- Sago topped ice desserts

TIP

● Though it's open 24-hours, this isn't the best late-night hawker hub in Singapore. Try to visit between 6pm and 8pm.

Choosing the best place to enjoy Singapore's legendary street food may seem futile, such are the options. However, if you only make it to one hawker food center, make it this one.

Setting Lau Pa Sat's appeal is as much about architecture and accessibility as it is about good food. Located at the point where Chinatown and the glitzy Central Business District (CBD) collide, the food area is housed within the largest remaining Victorian cast-iron building in Asia. It was built in 1894 on the site of an earlier outdoor wet market (the name means "old market" in Hokkien) and remains a magnificently ornate structure. Columns and embellished arches hold up the gazebo from which ceiling fans hang, the clock tower chimes on the hour, and the forecourt teems to the sound of cooking and feasting.

Nighttime By day Lau Pa Sat caters to the office crowd from the CBD but has more local color by night. The more than 100 food stalls range from Malay, through Indian to Chinese. However, satay snacks remain the most popular specialty. Boon Tat Street, alongside, is closed to traffic in the evenings when pushcarts hawking satay, *teh tarik* (hand-pulled milk tea), barbequed meats and seafood line the street. Back in the main building itself, there is a great dessert and drink counter where you can buy Singapore's famed ice-snacks .

Tuck in The food, as at all of the hawker areas, is very cheap and all tables are communal.

The museum is housed in a colonial building (left); exhibits in the film gallery (right)

Originally opened at the Raffles Museum and Library in 1887, this palatial structure has been transformed into one of Asia's truly great museums with a fantastic multimedia history exhibition.

Revamped Reopened in December 2006 after a major renovation, the former Singapore History Museum is now a must-visit destination. The appeal goes beyond the sumptuous colonial building and expertly curated exhibitions. The real reason to visit is the Singapore History Gallery where the country's past sparks to life.

History gallery Singapore's documented history may be brief, but this tale never gets bogged down. Precolonial history in dispensed within a single gallery, which includes the Singapore Stone, a lump of 1,000-year-old rock inscribed with a language that has never been deciphered. Then visitors are asked to choose between two pathways through the museum. One tells Singapore's story from the point of view of Everyman, the other introduces the characters who have shaped the nation's development. Both are fascinating.

The accompanying audio guide is key. By punching the numbers written on the museum floor into the gadget, visitors drive forward the narrative. The audio sometimes offers extra information, but there are also dramatizations of important scenes, or commentaries. The four lifestyle galleries are incredibly interactive and feature pared-down exhibitions on food, photography, fashion and film.

THE BASICS

www.nationalmuseum.sg

✚ E5

✉ 93 Stamford Road

☎ 6332 3659

🕐 History Gallery: daily 10–6 (last admission 5.30). Lifestyle Galleries: daily 10–8 (last entry 7.30)

🍴 Three excellent restaurants and an all-day café

🚇 Dhoby Gaut MRT 5 min. City Hall MRT 10 min

🚌 Many, including 7, 14, 16 and 36

♿ Good

💷 Moderate

❓ Free English language tours of the history gallery on some days

HIGHLIGHTS

● Singapore History Gallery
● The Singapore Stone
● Personal testimony from POWs interned by Japan
● Exhibition of Asia's herbs and spices in the Food Gallery

THE CITY ★ **TOP 25**

Little India

HIGHLIGHTS

- Sari shops
- Banana-leaf meals
- Fish-head curry
- Perfumed garlands
- Fortune-tellers
- Temples
- Spice shops
- Gold merchants

TIP

- The district comes alive with throngs of Singapore's Indian guest workers on Saturday nights.

Along Serangoon Road and the streets that surround it you can snatch all the sensations of India. Exotic aromas fill the air. Baskets overflow with spices. Stores are packed with colorful cloth.

Origins of Little India In the mid-19th century, lime pits and brick kilns were set up in the area, and it is thought that these attracted Singapore's Indians, who were laborers for the most part, to Serangoon Road. The swampy grasslands here were also good for raising cattle, another traditional occupation of the Indian community.

Little India today The district remains overwhelmingly Indian, full of sari-clad women, spice shops, jasmine-garland sellers, Hindu temples and restaurants. Architectural gems abound. Apart from

Clockwise from left: garland stall on Serangoon Road; banana leaf curry; browsing the shop stalls; gold shop on Serangoon Road; window shutters with garlands; Sri Veeramakaliamman Temple

the crowded, lively streets and the tempting food emporiums, there is also the Tekha (Zhujiao) Centre at the southern end of Serangoon Road, which has an excellent food center on the ground floor and clothes shops above. Across from the market, a little way up Serangoon Road, Komala Vilas restaurant (▷ 52) serves wonderful *dosai* (savory pancakes) and *thali* (mixed curries)—all vegetarian—as well as delicious Indian sweets such as milk *barfi*. Walk along Serangoon Road and you will come to Sri Veeramakaliamman Temple, dedicated to the ferocious goddess Kali. Farther on still is the Sri Srinivasa Perumal Temple, with its magnificent 1979 *gopuram* (ornamental gateway). Take a detour to Race Course Lane for a selection of Indian banana-leaf restaurants, notably those offering fish-head curry and a great selection of vegetable curries.

THE BASICS

www.littleindia.com.sg
✚ F4
✉ Serangoon Road
🍴 Many restaurants and cafés
🚇 Little India
🚌 8, 13, 20, 23, 26, 31, 64, 65, 66, 67, 81, 90, 97, 103, 106, 111, 125, 131, 133, 139, 142, 147, 151, 154, 865
♿ Free

Orchard Road

- Specialist shops
- Exclusive designer shops
- Coffee shops
- Centrepoint
- Books Kinokuniya
- Takashimaya
- Ngee Ann City

TIP

- Don't be tempted to jaywalk on this long road; look for the underground crossing points.

One of the world's great shopping boulevards, Orchard Road is the retail heart and soul of Singapore. Day or night, a stroll from one end to the other is a pleasure, even if you don't shop.

Room to move Wide sidewalks and plenty of potential coffee stops help make encountering the cosmopolitan charms of Orchard Road a pleasure. And escaping the extreme heat that this equatorial city experiences is as easy as dashing into one of the dozens of air-conditioned shopping malls that line the street. Goods from all parts of the world are on offer, including well-priced electrical items, designer fashions, antiques and gifts. Inexpensive food courts are prevalent and there are any number of good restaurants. For a fine walking tour, start at Centrepoint, near Somerset Station, and

Clockwise from left: Louis Vuitton store; ladies' fashion on display; Heeren Junction; Paragon Shopping Mall; Takashimaya store; bookshop in Takashimaya department store

walk to Tanglin Mall at the western end of the street. On the way, pause near the intersection with Scotts Road to drop in at Borders bookstore, or take in a film at the nearby Lido Cineplex.

Ngee Ann City Arguably the most impressive of Singapore's many shopping malls, this complex is especially popular because of its wide range of supplementary services: banks, restaurants, food courts, post office and supermarket. The stylish, pricey anchor store, Takashimaya, offers departmental shopping at its best, with lovely goods and Singapore's classiest food hall, where sushi is a top seller. Books Kinokuniya, Southeast Asia's largest bookstore, and the plethora of the top-of-the-line brand-name shops such as Chanel, Cartier and Tiffany, are additional draws. The plaza in front of the building buzzes on weekends.

THE BASICS

✚ E5 D5 C4
Ngee Ann City
www.nyeeancity.com.sg
✉ 391 Orchard Road
🕐 Daily 10–9.30. Restaurants on upper floors 10am–11pm
🍴 Restaurants, food courts, supermarket
🚇 Orchard
🚌 7, 14, 16, 65, 106, 111, 123, 167, 605
♿ Good 💲 Free
❓ Post office, with overseas delivery; customer service center; SISTIC outlet; banks

Raffles Hotel and Museum

Raffles Hotel exterior (left); the famous Singapore Sling (middle) and the courtyard (right)

THE BASICS

www.raffleshotel.com

+ F5

✉ 1 Beach Road

☎ 6337 1886

🍴 2 cafés, bakery, Chinese restaurant, grill, Tiffin room, deli and "fusion" restaurant

Ⓒ City Hall

🚌 14, 16, 36, 56, 82, 100, 107, 125, 167

♿ Good

❓ Free museum (🕐 Daily 10–7). Shopping arcade

HIGHLIGHTS

● Front facade
● Lobby
● Tiffin Room
● Bar and Billiard Room
● Singapore Sling
● Raffles Museum
● Palm Court
● Long Bar

The renovators may have tried too hard—the Long Bar, for instance, was repositioned to allow for a two-story bar to cater to the hordes of visitors—but Raffles remains one of the world's great heritage hotels.

Legend Say "Raffles" and you might conjure up an image of the very epitome of colonial style and service. Established by the Sarkies brothers in 1887, the hotel served the traders and travelers who, after the opening of the Suez Canal in 1869, were visiting the bustling commercial hub of Singapore in growing numbers.

Renowned establishment Within just a decade of opening, the original 10-room bungalow had been expanded and the two-story wings added. The main building was opened in 1899. Over the years the Raffles Hotel has acquired a worldwide reputation for fine service and food, with its charming blend of classical architecture and tropical gardens. The elegant Raffles Courtyard is at the back of the main building.

Past clients Over the years guests have included Somerset Maugham, Elizabeth Taylor, Noël Coward, Michael Jackson and Rudyard Kipling. The Raffles Museum is on the second floor, with Raffles Hotel memorabilia, a must-see for anyone nostalgic about the golden age of travel. The nearby Jubilee Hall presents a multimedia show on the hotel's history four times a day. Some 70 specialist shops adjoin the main building.

Singapore Art Museum

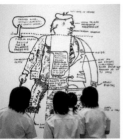

With its focus on art of the 20th century, this is Singapore's flagship art museum dedicated to the collection and display of contemporary works from Singapore and Southeast Asia. It also presents traveling exhibitions.

National treasure The museum, opened in 1996, is housed in the restored 19th-century St. Joseph's Institution building, a former Catholic boys' school, and displays Singapore's national art collection. The permanent collection has grown from less than 2,000 artworks to more than 6,000, and now houses the largest and most comprehensive collection of 20th-century Southeast Asian art in the region.

State of the art Almost 107,600sq ft (10,000sq m) of floor space includes 14 galleries, a reference library, an auditorium, a multipurpose hall, a museum shop, courtyards and an electronic E-image Gallery that runs interactive programs featuring some of the museum's collection on a large visual monitor. Check out the nearby café that looks out over Queens Street.

On show An overview of Singaporean art is on permanent display and traveling exhibitions expose the region internationally. A community program covers a diversity of art trends and practices, fringe activities and lectures. Check out Georgette Chen's striking *Self Portrait* (1934) and Chong Fah Cheong's tongue-in-cheek *Family and One* (1985).

THE BASICS

www.singart.com
 F5
✉ 71 Bras Basah Road
☎ 6332 3222
🕐 Daily 10–7 (Fri 10–9)
🍽 Café adjacent
Ⓜ Dhoby Ghaut, City Hall
🚌 14, 16, 36, 97, 124, 131, 162, 174
♿ Few
💲 Moderate; free admission Fri 6–9 and Mon–Fri 12–2
❓ Free guided tours Tue–Fri 11, 2, Sat, Sun 11, 2, 3.30. Museum shop

---

HIGHLIGHTS

● 19th-century building
● Large collection
● E-image Gallery
● Library
● Museum
● Temporary exhibitions

Singapore Flyer

25

The observation wheel (left); view from one of the cabins (right)

THE BASICS

www.singaporeflyer.com.sg

⊞ G6

✉ 30 Raffles Avenue

☎ 6333 3311

🕐 Daily 8.30am–10.30pm

🍴 Seafood, steak, Mexican, Japanese, among others

🚍 From Raffles Hotel (by City Hall MRTP) take bus 111, 106 or 133. A free shuttle return to City Hall is provided to ticket holders

♿ Good

💰 Expensive

❓ The security procedures are similar to an airport, and it's best to allow up to 30 min to collect tickets and pass through the check-points. For an extral SGD 40, you can enjoy a cocktail during your flight

HIGHLIGHTS

● Views as far as Malaysia and Indonesia on clear days
● Singapore's sparkling night skyline
● Yakult Rainforest Discovery Park

Opened to great fanfare in spring 2008, the world's largest observation wheel offers a spectacular perspective on the urban heart of Singapore, with Malaysia and Indonesia also visible on clear days.

Orientation Perched on the edge of the developing Marina, and climbing to an impressive 165m (541ft), the Singapore Flyer is the latest addition to the skyline. The ever-changing perspective and pedestrian speed make it the best way to familiarize yourself with the layout below.

Panoramic views The ride lasts around 35 minutes and begins with views back across the Marina to the skyscrapers of the Central Business District. This angle also offers a great overview of the huge construction projects taking place around the Marina—including Singapore's first casino, part of the gargantuan Las Vegas Sands complex, slated to open in 2009. The comedown focuses attention on the north of the city, taking in Kampung Glam, Little India and the northeastern districts of Geylang and Katong.

The ride Each air-conditioned capsule accommodates up to 28 people. There are two screens in each capsule but, disappointingly, these broadcast adverts and slack-bass funk music, rather than any commentary on the landmarks (though you will be informed when you've reached the top of the ride). There's also a three-story airport terminal-style building at the base of the wheel, featuring shopping and dining options.

More to See

ARAB STREET

Good handicrafts from all over Asia can be bought near the intersection of Beach Road and Arab Street, where some of the area's original shops still survive. Look for basketware, textiles, lace, silverwork, jewelry and perfume. This is the best area in Singapore for buying fabric; numerous shops offer silks, cottons and batiks.

➕ G4/5 ✉ Between North Bridge Road and Beach Road 🚇 Bugis

BUGIS STREET

Bugis Street was rebuilt in 1991, 449ft (137m) from its original site. It's two sections, either side of Victoria Street, contrast sharply. The western stretch is most fun and contains the largest covered outdoor market in town (as well as possibly the largest ceiling fan on earth). There are clothes, crafts, curios, as well as fake luxury goods and snacks and drinks. There are heaps of fruit and veg stalls near Albert Street. Bugis Street east of Victoria Street is dominated by the Bugis Junction shopping plaza, a collection of brand name shops and indie stores in air-conditioned surrounds.

➕ F5 ✉ Bugis Street 🕐 Outdoor market open daily until midnight. Bars open daily to 2 or 3am 🍴 Fast-food outlets 🚇 Bugis 🚌 2, 5, 7, 12, 32, 61, 62, 63, 84, 130, 160, 197, 520, 851, 960 ♿ Few (pedestrian precinct) ✋ Moderate bars and food, antiques and crafts

CHETTIAR'S TEMPLE

The temple of Sri Thandayuthanapani, rebuilt in 1984, is also called Chettiar's Temple after the Indian *chettiars* (moneylenders) who financed its construction in the 1850s. The *gopuram* is a riot of images and colors. Each glass panel of the unusual 48-panel ceiling frieze, from India, features a deity from the Hindu pantheon.

➕ E6 ✉ 15 Tank Road ☎ 6737 9393 🕐 Daily 8–12, 5.30–8.30 🚇 Dhoby Ghaut ✋ Free

DHL BALLOON

www.ducktours.com.sg
Not to be outdone by the new Singapore Flyer, the DHL Balloon, a

THE CITY ★ MORE TO SEE

Outside Chettiar Temple

Arab Street shop display

new tethered helium balloon ride, upped its maximum flight height from 150 meters to 180 meters, making it the tallest of Singapore's three major sightseeing lookouts. The casket is less a creaking wicker basket than a circular steel gangway, but it does make it possible to get a great angle on every part of the city state, and there's a peculiar thrill in the slight swaying of the balloon. The 180m (590ft) flight costs more than the standard 150m (492ft) flight, and the journey lasts less than 15 minutes.

✚ F5 ✉ Tan Quee Lan Street ☎ 6338 6877 🕐 Daily 11.30am–9.30pm 🍴 Bar food and drinks on-site 🚇 Bugis MRT 5-min walk ♿ Good 💷 Expensive ❓ The balloon is sensitive to adverse weather conditions and is often grounded

MINT MUSEUM OF TOYS
www.emint.com

This new five-floor museum brings in toys from 25 countries, including some rare and valuable antiques up to a century old. The exhibitions will likely induce nostalgia among big kids and high excitement among adult collectors, though there's educational value for younger visitors with some hands-on displays. The museum's café is more a restaurant proper and does pricy dishes with a fine wine collection. There are also collectables on hand, thematically linked to the toys in the main exhibition.

✚ F5 ✉ 26 Seah Street ☎ 6339 0660 🕐 Daily 9.30–6.30 🍴 Café 🚇 City Hall, Bugis MRT ♿ Good 💷 Moderate

MUSEUM OF SHANGHAI TOYS
www.most.com.sg

The world's first museum to exclusively show toys originating from China, the compact museum has three levels of exhibition space. Look out for such delightful and nostalgic exhibits as an electric tram from the 1920s, an Ada Lunn Doll dating from the1950s, and an ethnic doll from the1960s. There is a souvenir and retail shop on the ground floor.

✚ F4 ✉ 83 Rowell Road ☎ 6294 7747 🕐 Mon–Sun 10–8 🚇 Farrer Park ♿ Good 💷 Moderate

Mickey Mouse exhibit at the Mint Museum of Toys

Padang baseball player

THE PADANG

Once the Padang directly faced the sea, but land reclamation in Marina Bay has long since changed its outlook. This huge rectangular lawn, which goes back to Raffles' days, has retained its use as a recreational area. Cricket and rugby matches are played in season and while nonmembers may not venture into the clubs, they can stand and watch the games. City Hall, facing the Padang, has seen several historic events: the herding of Europeans onto the Padang on the morning of the Japanese occupation, and the formal surrender of the Japanese on its steps in 1945. At the southern end is the Cricket Club, with a commanding view of the Padang. The group of government buildings includes the attorney-general's chambers (resembling a small opera house), the Victoria Theatre and Concert Hall buildings, and the former Parliament House.

➕ F6 ✉ St. Andrew's Road 🚇 City Hall 🚌 10, 70, 75, 82, 97, 100, 107, 125, 130, 131, 167, 196 ♿ None 🎫 Free

PERANAKAN MUSEUM

www.peranakanmuseum.sg

This excellent new museum is on the site of the original Asian Civilisations Museum at the edge of Fort Canning Park. It documents Singapore's most fascinating minority race, the Peranakans. This slightly slippery term refers to descendents of mixed-race marriages between Malays and Chinese or Indian settlers. The displays focus mainly on the Chinese Peranakan culture. The first floor is given over to Peranakan wedding rituals, with more focused exhibits on fashion, eating and religion on the second floor—and make for a fascinating insight into how the Peranakans, and Singaporeans, have learned to blend cultures. To better understand the meaning of "Peranakan," begin your visit by watching the talking heads video on the second floor.

➕ E5/6 ✉ 39 Armenian Street ☎ 6332 7591 🕐 Mon 1–7, Tue–Sun 9.30–7 (open till 9 on Fri) 🍴 Restaurants and cafés nearby 🚇 City Hall MRT, 5 min ♿ Good 🎫 Inexpensive. Free Fri 7–9

Wedding chamber in the Peranakan Museum

RED DOT MUSEUM

www.red-dot.sg

Housed within a striking scarlet-washed colonial building that once played home to the Singaporean traffic police, the red dot design museum is a fascinating new exhibition space that showcases award winners from Germany's highly-respected red dot organization. The displays are divided between imaginative design concepts, yet to be given commercial backing, and finished products that have set the standard in their field, spanning everything from mechanized gadgetry to children's toys. Despite the size of the building, this is not a huge space, divided between one large industrial room and a spotlighted gallery. However, it's only one of two of its kind in the world and will delight creatives or thinkers without using up too much time.

🚼 E8 🖾 GF, Red Dot Traffic Building, 28 Maxwell Road ☎ 6327 8027 🕐 Mon, Tue, Fri, 11–6, Sat, Sun 11–8 🍴 Maxwell Road Food Centre nearby 🚇 Tanjong Pagar MRT 3-min walk 🔥 Good 🖐 Moderate

❓ Occasionally closed for private events so call ahead

SRI MARIAMMAN TEMPLE

This is Singapore's oldest Hindu temple, a Technicolor shrine with brilliant statuary on the tower. The first temple, erected in 1827, was made of wood and atap (nipa-palm leaves). The temple is dedicated to the goddess Mariamman, said to have powers to cure epidemics such as cholera and smallpox. The temple shows the three principal elements of Dravidian architecture: an interior shrine (*vimanam*) covered by a decorated dome, an assembly hall (*madapam*) used for prayers and an entrance tower (*gopuram*) covered with painted Hindu deities. The preferred venue of most Hindu weddings, the temple is still very much a place of worship and you must respect this and remember to remove your footwear before entering.

🚼 E7 🖾 244 South Bridge Road ☎ 6223 4064 🕐 Daily 7am–9pm 🚇 Chinatown 🚌 SBS bus 103, 166, 167 from City Hall 🔥 None 🖐 Free

The red dot museum

Statue in the Sri Mariamman Temple

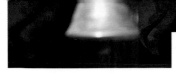

Around Singapore's Historic Core

Get a feel for both the old and new Singapore with this long walk that includes temples and the grand Raffles Hotel.

DISTANCE: 5 miles (8km) **ALLOW:** 5 hours

START

MAXWELL ROAD
✚ E7 🚇 Tanjong Pagar

END

ARAB STREET
✚ G4 🚇 Bugis

❶ From Maxwell Road walk down South Bridge Road to visit the Buddha Tooth Relic Temple (▷ 26). Turn left down South Street and return to South Bridge Road via Trengganu and Padoga streets..

❷ Note the renovated Chinese shophouses and visit the Sri Mariamman Temple (▷ 44). Cross over and take Ann Siang Hill, then turn left down Club Street.

❸ Turn right at Cross Street and left into Telok Ayer Street. Far East Square and China Square are full of places to eat. Check out Fuk Tak Chi Museum.

❹ Turn right down Cheang Hong Lim Place and left at the end of Chruch Street and follow Market Street and Malacca Place in Raffles Place. head north to reach Bonham Street and turn left into Boat Quay.

❽ Wander around the streets lined with old shops selling cloth and handicrafts. Return to your hotel.

❼ After Raffles City is Raffles Hotel (▷ 38). Continue along Beach Road. Turn left into Arab Street, right into Baghdad Street and left into Bussorah Street. Facing Sultan Mosque, take the side street to your left, then head up Arab Street to Victoria Street.

❻ Cross and pass Empress Place on the riverside promenade before turning right into Old Parliament Lane to pass the Victoria Concert Hall and Theatre. On the right is Singapore Cricket Club. Cross over High Street and take St. Andrew's road. The Padang is on your right.

❺ Walk along the riverbank until you come to Cavenagh Bridge.

THE CITY

WALK

45

Shopping

APPLE CENTRE AT FUNAN

Mac fans can now get a good range of Apple products, including the iPod.

🔲 F6 ✉ 05-07 Funan IT Mall, 109 North Bridge Road ☎ 6336 9929 🕐 Mon–Fri 11–8, Sat, Sun 12–7 🚇 City Hall

CATHAY PHOTO STORE

Carries a great range of traditional and digital cameras and accessories. Knowledgable staff. You can haggle a bit here.

🔲 G6 ✉ 2-215/216 Marina Square, 6 Raffles Boulevard ☎ 6339 6188 🕐 Daily 9–11 🚇 City Hall

CENTREPOINT

www.fraserscentrepointmalls.com

One of the most user-friendly complexes, with good department stores (Robinson's and Marks & Spencer) and shops selling everything from books to clothes and electrical goods, plus restaurants and a supermarket.

🔲 D5 ✉ 176 Orchard Road ☎ 6737 9000 🕐 Daily 10–10 🚇 Somerset

CHINATOWN POINT

One of Chinatown's earliest shopping centers, containing a variety of shops and eateries, and specializing in local handicraft and gift shops.

🔲 E7 ✉ 133 New Bridge Road ☎ 6534 5767

🕐 Mon–Fri 9–4.30, Sat 9–12 🚇 Outram Park

FUNAN DIGITALIFE MALL

www.funan.com.sg

A huge range of computers and accessories, as well as photographic equipment.

🔲 F6 ✉ 109 North Bridge Road ☎ 6336 8327 🕐 Daily 10.30–8.30 🚇 City Hall

THE HEEREN

www.heeren.com.sg

Popular among the hip and trendy. Browse the three floors of HMV (present your passport at customer services to get a discount card) or sip coffee at Spinelli's outdoor café.

🔲 D5 ✉ 260 Orchard Road ☎ 6733 4725 🕐 Daily 10am–11pm 🚇 Somerset

LUCKY PLAZA

www.luckyplazashopping.com

Another huge shopping complex, full of small shops selling all manner

---

HONG BAO

You may notice small red packets on sale. These *hong bao*, as they are known, are used for giving gifts of money, particularly for weddings and at Chinese New Year, when it is the custom for unmarried children to receive a red packet. Many employers also choose this time of year to give their red packets–bonuses.

---

of goods. Salespeople may be aggressive, so bargain hard.

🔲 D5 ✉ 304 Orchard Road ☎ 6235 3294 🕐 Daily 10–7 (but individual shop times vary) 🚇 Orchard

MILLENIA WALK

More than 190 designer and street-smart fashion stores and specialty shops, such as Raoul, jewelers like the Hour Glass and Cortina E'space, and electrical superstore Harvey Norman.

🔲 G6 ✉ 9 Raffles Boulevard ☎ 6883 1122 🕐 Daily 11–9 generally 🚇 City Hall

MUSTAFA CENTRE

More than 75,000 items over four floors in Singapore's only 24-hour mall. Clothing, CDs, jewelry and cameras are among the universe of choices. Great for bargain-hunters.

🔲 F3 ✉ 145 Syed Alwi Road ☎ 6295 5855 🕐 24 hours, 7 days 🚇 Farrer Park

PEOPLE'S PARK COMPLEX

You can buy all manner of goods at this bustling complex in the heart of Chinatown, including traditional remedies and Asian textiles. There are plenty of clothing and electronic shops, too. This is one of the city's oldest shopping centers.

🔲 E7 ✉ 1 Park Road ☎ 6535 9533 🕐 Daily 10–9.45 🚇 Outram Park

PIDEMCO CENTRE

The Pidemco Centre, home of the Singapore Jewellery Mart, is a good starting point to get an overview of the range and cost of jewelry available here.
⊞ E7 ⊠ 95 South Bridge Road ◷ Mon–Sat 10.30–6 Ⓜ City Hall

RAFFLES CITY

www.rafflescity.com
Fresh from a huge revamp, the four-story mall section of this IM Pei-designed "city within a city" has individual floors dedicated to luxury buyers, fashionistas and children. It's maybe Singapore's most accessible mall, with access from the City Hall interchange.
⊞ G4 ⊠ 252 North Bridge Road ☎ 6338 7766 ◷ Daily 10–9.30 Ⓜ City Hall

SINGAPORE HANDICRAFT CENTRE

Five floors of shops in the heart of Chinatown, where you can find all manner of curios, including antique snuff bottles, carpets and calligraphic works.
⊞ E7 ⊠ Chinatown Point, 133 New Bridge Road ◷ Mon–Fri 9–4.30, Sat 9–12 Ⓜ Outram Park

SUNTEC CITY MALL

www.sunteccity.com.sg
One of Singapore's largest shopping malls, divided into four zones: Galleria, Tropics, Entertainment Centre and Fountain Terrace. Features brand-name stores and specialty shops, including the G2000 flagship store and Mango, and French hypermarket Carrefour.
⊞ G5 ⊠ 3 Temasek Boulevard ☎ 6825 2667 ◷ Daily 10–10 Ⓜ City Hall

TANGS

www.tangs.com
This popular department store has shelf after shelf of fashions and accessories.
⊞ C4 ⊠ 320 Orchard Road ☎ 6737 5500 ◷ Mon–Thu 10.30–9.30, Fri–Sat 10.30–11, Sun 11–8.30 Ⓜ Orchard

TEMPLE/PAGODA/ TRENGGANU STREETS

In the streets between South Bridge Road and New Bridge Road, in the heart of Chinatown, shops and stalls sell a tantalizing range of Chinese goods: herbal

BARGAINING

Many Singapore shopkeepers are happy for you to bargain with them and it can save you a significant percentage, even on fairly small purchases. Don't make your first offer until the seller has reduced the opening price at least once. It is considered a matter of honor that once you have settled on a price, you must go through with the deal. Don't bargain if you see "Fixed price" signs.

remedies, porcelain, exotic fruit and gold jewelry. The rich smell of a Chinese favorite, barbecued pork, pervades the streets.
⊞ E7 ⊠ Off South Bridge Road Ⓜ Chinatown

THIEVES MARKET

The ultimate bargain haunt in Singapore, with lots of down at heel vendors selling second-hand goods from tarpaulin on the pavement. Bargaining is essential, and things only get into full swing after sundown.
⊞ F5 ⊠ Sngei Road ◷ Daily 11am–10pm approx Ⓜ Bugis

VIVOCITY

www.vivocity.com.sg
Singapore's biggest malls a stunning retail and leisure complex on the waterfront, with department stores and brand-name shops, plus cinemas and a hypermarket.
⊞ B9 ⊠ 1 Harbourfront Walk C6377 6860 ◷ Daily 10–10 Ⓜ Harbourfront

YUE HWA CHINESE PRODUCTS EMPORIUM

This well laid-out department store in the heart of Chinatown has an extensive array of quality merchandise, from traditional and modern clothes to handicrafts, food and household items.
⊞ E7 ⊠ 70 Eu Tong Sen Street ☎ 6538 4222 ◷ Daily 11–9 Ⓜ Chinatown

Entertainment and Nightlife

LE BAROQUE
Part bohemian, part sophisticate, exuberant Le Baroque features electrifying live music from local rock icon Douglas Oliveiro and Satellite. This bar, nightspot and restaurant's modern Gothic decor features wrought-iron chandeliers, baroque-style paintings, a Roman column and gold tinged walls, and the washrooms have boudoir appeal.
➕ F5 ✉ 1-07 Fountain Court, Chijmes, 30 Victoria Street ☎ 6339 6696 🕙 Mon–Thu 11–11, Fri 11am–1am, Sat 9am–1am, Sun 9am–11pm 🚇 City Hall

BLU JAZ CAFÉ
www.blujaz.net
A friendly, laid-back jazz spot at the southern edge of Kampong Glam, just off Haji Lane. There's live music nightly after 9pm.
➕ G5 ✉ 11 Bali Lane, Kampong Glam ☎ 6292 3800 🚇 Bugis 🕙 Mon–Thu noon–midnight, Fri noon–2am, Sat 3pm–2am

CARNEGIE'S
This lively bar, with its emphasis on rock music and occasional bar-top dancing, is favored by locals and expats alike.
➕ E8 ✉ 44–45 Pekin Street, Far East Square ☎ 6534 0850 🕙 Tue–Fri 11am–2am, Sat 5pm–3am, Sun 5pm–midnight 🚇 Raffles Place

THE DUBLINER IRISH PUB
Set in a former colonial mansion, this popular pub, with its plush interior, serves excellent food.
➕ E5 ✉ 165 Penang Road ☎ 6735 2220 🕙 Daily noon–2am 🚇 Dhoby Ghaut

HARRY'S QUAYSIDE
A riverside location close to the city makes this one of Singapore's most popular places for a drink, and the crowd often spills out onto the sidewalk. Blues on Sunday, jazz Wednesday to Saturday.
➕ E6 ✉ 28 Boat Quay ☎ 6538 3029 🕙 Mon–Thu 11am–midnight, Fri, Sat 11am–3am, Sun 11am–1am 🚌 16, 31, 55

HELIPAD
www.helipad.com.sg
Singapore's latest rooftop bar-cum-club is a luxe, trendy affair. Helipad occupies the top two levels of the central building, with the alfresco deck on the upper level great for views and soaking up champagne.
➕ E6 ✉ 05-22 The Central, 6 Eu Tong Sen Street ☎ 6327 8118 🕙 Mon–Thu 6pm–1am, Fri–Sat 6pm–3am. Happy hour 6–9pm 🚇 Clark Quay

LONG BAR AND BAR & BILLARDS ROOM
The Singapore Sling is usually high on a visitor's list of things to taste in Singapore, and the place to enjoy it is undoubtedly the Bar and Billiards Room and the Long Bar, both in the Raffles Hotel (▷ 38), where the drink was first served.
➕ F5 ✉ Raffles Hotel Arcade ☎ 6337 1886 🕙 Sun–Thu 11am–1am, Fri, Sat 6pm–2am 🚇 City Hall

LOOF
The most famous rooftop bar in Singapore is an eccentric, artsy affair and majors in down tempo electronica. One for budding artists, designers and fashionistas.
➕ G4 ✉ 03-07 Odean Towers, 331 North Bridge Road ☎ 6338 8035 🕙 Mon–Fri 5.30pm–2am, Sat, Sun 5.30pm–3am 🚇 City Hall

MINISTRY OF SOUND
www.ministryofsound.com.sg
Progressive house, funky beats, electro, hip-hop/R&B, disco and soulful house from a multimillion

WHAT'S ON
Concerts and theater are very popular, particularly for weekend shows. Details of events, their venues and where to buy tickets can be found in Singapore's daily morning newspaper, the *Straits Times*, and various free publications. Tickets are obtainable from SISTIC and TicketCharge outlets at Centrepoint, Tanglin Mall, Wisma Atria, Great World City, Raffles City Shopping Centre, Takashimaya Store, Funan Centre, Junction 8 and Bugis Junction. Bookings ☎ 6348 5555 and 6296 2929.

dollar sound system complemented by digital imaging projectors and special effects machines.
➕ E6 ✉ Block 3C, The Cannery, River Valley Road, Clarke Quay ☎ 6333 4168 🖐 S$25 inclusive of 2 house-pour drinks ⏰ Wed–Sat 9pm–4am

NEW ASIA BAR

The New Asia Bar boasts the best views in town, and has surprisingly reasonably priced cocktails during the Sundowners promotion between 5 and 9pm, Thursday to Sunday. It's great for a drink at dusk.
➕ F6 ✉ 72F, The Swissotel, 2 Stamford Road ☎ 6837 3322 ⏰ Sun–Wed 3pm–1am, Thu–Sat 3pm–3am 🚇 City Hall ❓ Dress code after 9pm

PALONG LOBBY BAR

Located in the Rendezvous Hotel, you get great cocktails in tranquil surroundings.
➕ E5 ✉ 9 Bras Basah Road ☎ 6335 1880 ⏰ Daily noon–midnight (Fri, Sat 1am) 🚇 Dhoby Ghaut

PAPA JOE'S

This vibrant nightspot, with a great Orchard Road location, is popular with locals and expats alike. Enjoy Tex-Mex food with a Mediterranean twist. The mango margaritas are legendary. Great pizzas.
➕ D5 ✉ 180 Orchard Road ☎ 6732 6966 ⏰ Daily 5pm–3am 🚇 Somerset

PAULANER BRAHAUS

Serves Authentic Bavarian cuisine and popular Munich beer in a range of types. The rustic setting is reminiscent of German microbreweries.
➕ F6 ✉ 01–01 Tone Square @ Millennia Walk, 9 Raffles Boulevard ☎ 6883 2572 ⏰ Sun–Thu 11.30am–1am, Fri, Sat 11.30am–2am 🚌 32, 54, 195 🚇 City Hall

POST BAR

Part of the stylish Fullerton hotel (▷ 112), this bar serves classic and fruity cocktails.
➕ F6 ✉ 1 Fullerton Square ☎ 6877 8135 ⏰ Mon–Fri noon–2am, Sat, Sun 5pm–2am 🚇 Raffles Place

---

ONE FOR THE ROAD

After working a 10- to 12-hour day, your average Singaporean either heads home to relax with family members, or, if they are young and single, stops at a favorite bar for a drink en route. Weekends see increased nightlife activity; clubs do a roaring trade and attract expats and locals alike, especially those in the courting mode. As in other large cities, there is a good selection of Irish pubs and October brings a quota of German-inspired beer fests. And don't leave the city without having a Singapore Sling at the famous Long Bar at Raffles Hotel (▷ 38).

THE PUMP ROOM

www.pumproomasia.com
A combined microbrewery, bistro and bar, Pump Room is one of Clarke Quay's hot-spots come night time A live band plays pop, rock and jazz every day but Monday.
➕ E6 ✉ Block B, River Valley Road, Clark Quay ☎ 6334 2628 ⏰ Mon–Sat noon–3am, Sun 10.30am–3am 🚇 Clarke Quay

SOUTHBRIDGE JAZZ

www.southbridgejazz.com.sg
This is a slick and intimate jazz venue. The house band plays every night, but big-name shows occur regularly.
➕ E6 ✉ 82 Boat Quay ☎ 6327 4671 ⏰ Tue–Sun 5.30pm–1am (Sat, Sun 2am) 🚇 Clarke Quay

VICTORIA THEATRE AND CONCERT HALL

Classical and other concerts take place here Check local media for peformance details.
➕ E5 ✉ 11 Empress Place ☎ 6338 1230 🚇 Raffles Place

ZOUK

This is Singapore's most famous club. Excellent in-house and guest DJs spin the discs. It's in a converted godown near the River View Hotel, next to Phuture and Velvet Underground, all three expensive.
➕ D6 ✉ 17–21 Jiak Kim Street ☎ 6738 2988 ⏰ Daily 7pm–3am 🚌 16

Restaurants

PRICES

Prices are approximate, based on a 3-course meal for one person.

$$$	over S$50
$$	S$20–S$50
$	under S$20

BENG THIN HOON KEE ($)

Hokkien food is popular in Singapore, for the ancestors of many Singaporeans lived in southern China, where the cuisine originated. Try duck in lotus leaves.
➕ F7 ✉ 05–02 OCBC Building, 65 Chulia Street ☎ 6533 7708 🕔 Daily 11.30–3, 6–10 🚇 Raffles Place

BLUE GINGER ($$)

Set in an old shophouse, this is the best place in Singapore to try Peranakan dishes such as fried pork and prawn rolls, *ayam panggang* (chicken in coconut milk) and durian desserts.
➕ E8 ✉ 97 Tanjong Pagar Road, Chinatown ☎ 6222 3928 🕔 Daily 12–2.30, 6.30–10 🚇 Tanjong Pagar

CHINA SQUARE ($)

This sprawling three-floor food complex has Western food outlets and traditional hawker fare under one roof.
➕ E7 ✉ 51 Telok Ayer Street 🕔 Daily 7am–10pm 🚇 Tanjong Pagar

CHINATOWN FOOD STREET ($)

This side street is lined with open-air (but canvas-covered) stalls that come into their own after dark. Most types of local Chinese food are available plus a range of desserts—try the ice *kacang*.
➕ E7 ✉ Smith Street 🕔 Early until late, daily 🚇 Chinatown

THE CHOCOLATE FACTORY

This gourmet chocolate shop and café has a scenic location on the Singapore River at Robertson Quay. Pastries, pralines and freshly made cakes are among the rich treats on the menu.
➕ D6 ✉ Unit 11, The Pier, Robertson Quay, 80 Mohamed

SATAY

No trip to Singapore would be complete without the famous satay, a Malay dish. Sticks of chicken, lamb or beef, and sometimes other foods such as tofu, are barbecued and served with a thick, sweet peanut sauce. Small rice cakes and cucumber usually accompany the satay. It is served in some restaurants, and at many hawker centers there is a "satay man." If you develop a taste for it, look in supermarkets for the ready-made satay sauce and try it at home with a barbecue.

Sultan Road ☎ 6235 9007 🕔 Mon–Thu 1–10.30pm; Fri–Sun 1–11.30pm 🚌 16

CRYSTAL JADE ($$)

www.crystaljade.com
Traditional Cantonese cuisine including fresh seafood dishes, barbecued pork and soups. This Asia-wide chain also serves arguably the best dim sum in town
➕ C4 ✉ 27 Ngee Ann City, 391 Orchard Road ☎ 6238 1661 🕔 Daily 11.30–2.30, 6.30–10.30 🚇 Orchard

HAE BOK'S KOREAN RESTAURANT ($$)

Reliably good Korean dishes such as fried octopus with Korean spicy sauce and fried, egg-coated vegetables.
➕ E8 ✉ 44–46 Tanjong Pagar Road ☎ 6223 9003 🕔 Daily 11.30–3, 5.30–10 🚇 Tanjong Pagar

INDOCHINE ($$$)

The original haunt of what is now a global restaurant and bar brand is tucked away in Chinatown. Vietnamese/Cambodian/Laotian dishes include spicy sausage and fried fish. There are four other branches in Singapore, including the lavish Forbidden City at Clarke Quay.
➕ E7 ✉ 49B Club Street ☎ 6323 0503 🕔 Mon–Fri 12–3, 6.30–11, Sat 6.30–12 🚇 Chinatown

KOMALA VILAS ($)

www.komalavilas.com.sg
Vegetarian Indian fare is served here on banana leaves. It's good and inexpensive, and you can have unlimited helpings. For a different drink, try the sweet, spicy *masala* tea.

✚ F4 ⊠ 76–78 Serangoon Road ☎ 6293 6980 🕐 Daily 11–3.30, 6–10.30 🚇 Bugis

PASTA BRAVA ($$)

A lovely Italian restaurant in a converted shophouse on the edge of Chinatown. Some dishes can be expensive, but the food is very good. This place is popular with workers at lunch.

✚ E8 ⊠ 11 Craig Road ☎ 6227 7550 🕐 Daily 11.30–2.30, 6.30–10.30 🚇 Tanjong Pagar

PAULANER BRÄUHAUS ($$)

www.paulaner.com.sg
German theme restaurant-cum-brewery serving generous platters of *sauerkraut* and *wurst kartoffeln*.

✚ F6 ⊠ 01 Millennia Walk, 9 Raffles Boulevard ☎ 6883 2572 🕐 Daily 12–2.30, 6.30–10.30 (drinks only after 10) 🚇 City Hall

PETE'S PLACE ($$$)

This basement trattoria is popular with both visitors and locals. The pastas are tasty and an excellent salad bar makes the place a good bet for vegetarians.

✚ C4 ⊠ Basement, Grand Hyatt Hotel, 10–12 Scotts Road ☎ 6730 7113 🕐 Daily 1.30–2.30, 6–11 🚇 Orchard

PREGO ($$$)

This long-established restaurant bustles at lunch and in the evenings thanks to an excellent range of dishes and a perfect central location.

✚ F6 ⊠ Westin Stamford Hotel, 2 Stamford Road ☎ 6431 5156 🕐 Daily 11.30–2.30, 6.30–10.30 🚇 City Hall

RANG MAHAL ($$$)

This restaurant has moved to the ultramodern Pan Pacific Hotel but is still serving a good range of North Indian dishes and an extensive lunch and dinner buffet. Indian dancers perform.

✚ G6 ⊠ Level 3, Pan Pacific Hotel, Raffles Boulevard ☎ 6333 1788 🕐 Daily 12–2.30, 6.30–10.30 🚇 City Hall

---

POPIAH

Popiah—freshly prepared rice-flour pancakes filled with a mouthwatering mixture of onion, turnip, bean sprouts, minced pork and prawns, all held together with a sweet soy sauce and flavored with coriander, garlic and chili—makes a delicious snack. You can order *popiah* in some restaurants, and many hawker centers have a *popiah* stall.

RESTAURANT EMBER

This small and hip restaurant is part of the boutique backpackers joint, Hotel 1929. Singaporean chef Sebastian Ng serves up both straight-laced European dishes and racy fusion concoctions.

✚ E6 ⊠ Ground floor, Hotel 1929, 50 Keong Saik Road ☎ 63471928 🕐 Mon–Fri, 11.30am–2pm, 6.30–10pm, Sat 6.30–10pm 🚇 Outram Park

SRI VIJAYA ($)

Modest vegetarian, banana-leaf establishment offering great value with its generous helpings of rice and vegetable accompaniments.

✚ F4 ⊠ 229 Selegie Road ☎ 6336 1748 🕐 Daily 9–9 🚇 Bugis

SUPERNATURE ($)

Soy burgers, healthy sandwiches and fresh juices are the staples at this chic organic shop. Vegans well catered to.

✚ C5 ⊠ 01–21 Park House, 21 Orchard Boulevard ☎ 6735 4338 🕐 Mon–Sat 10–7, Sun 11–6 🚇 Orchard

ZAMBUCCA ($$$)

Italian favorite with retro decor and lighting. House specialties include baked black cod and prawns, and foie gras with apple compote and port wine jus.

✚ G6 ⊠ Third floor, Pan Pacific Hotel, Raffles Boulevard ☎ 6337 8086 🕐 Daily 11.30am–2.30pm, 6pm–10.30pm 🚇 Marina Bay

Head west for the world's best bird park, a patch of the island's original tropical rainforest, and hedonistic Sentosa, fast becoming the recreational hub of this dynamic island nation.

Sights	**56–75**	Top 25	**TOP 25**
Walk	**76**	Botanic Gardens ▷ **56**	
		Jurong BirdPark ▷ **58**	
Shopping	**77**	Night Safari ▷ **60**	
		Sentosa ▷ **62**	
Restaurants	**78**	Singapore Discovery Centre ▷ **64**	
		Singapore Nature Reserves ▷ **66**	
		Singapore Science Centre ▷ **68**	
		Singapore Zoo ▷ **70**	

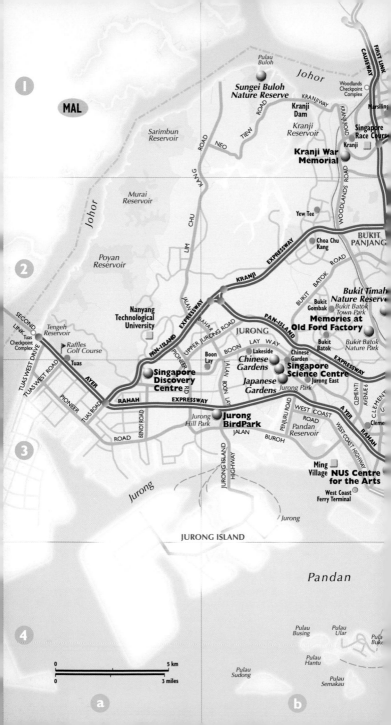

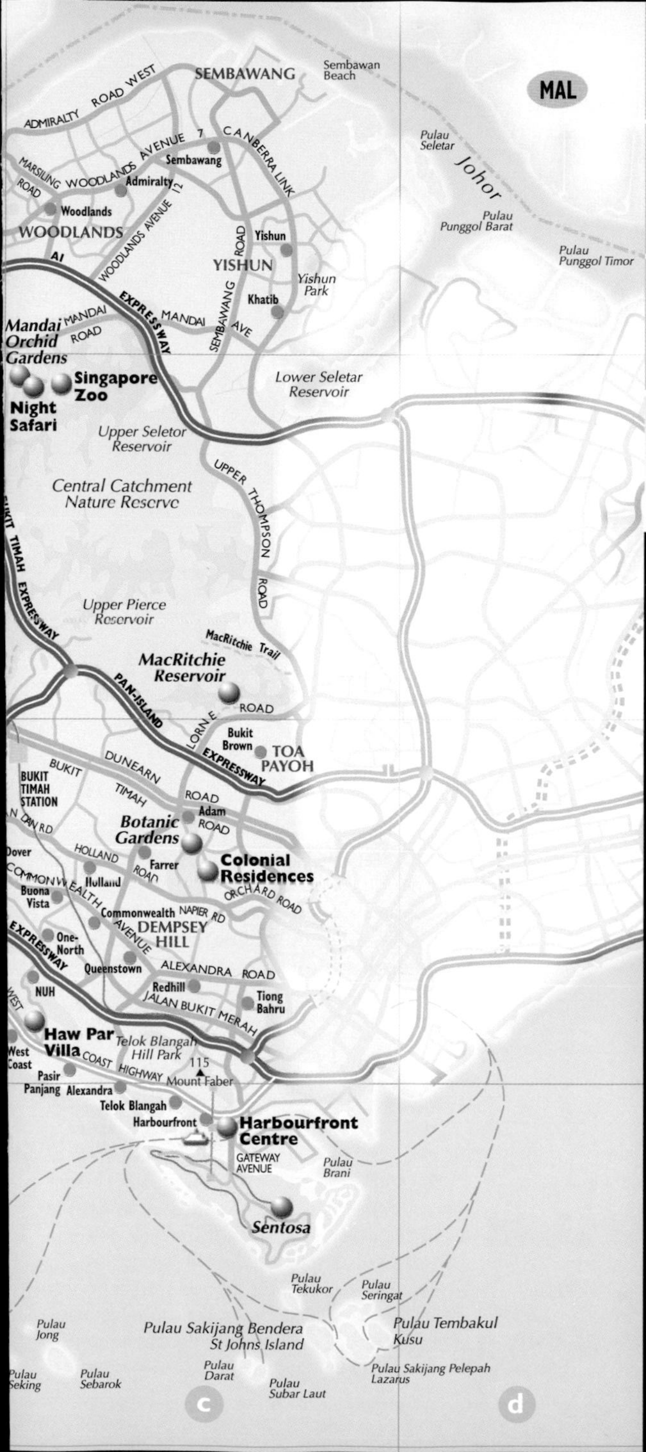

MAL

SEMBAWANG
Sembawan
Beach

ADMIRALTY ROAD WEST

MARSILING WOODLANDS AVENUE 7 CANBERRA LINK
ROAD
Sembawang
Admiralty

Pulau
Seletar

Johor

Pulau
Punggol Barat

Pulau
Punggol Timor

WOODLANDS AVENUE 2

WOODLANDS
Woodlands

AI

Yishun

YISHUN

Yishun
Park

Khatib

Mandai
Orchid
Gardens

MANDAI ROAD

MANDAI

EXPRESSWAY

SEMBAWANG AVE

Lower Seletar
Reservoir

Singapore
Zoo

Night
Safari

Upper Seletor
Reservoir

UPPER THOMPSON ROAD

Central Catchment
Nature Reserve

BUKIT TIMAH EXPRESSWAY

Upper Pierce
Reservoir

MacRitchie Trail

MacRitchie
Reservoir

PAN-ISLAND

LORN E ROAD

Bukit
Brown

EXPRESSWAY

TOA
PAYOH

BUKIT
TIMAH
STATION

DUNEARN

BUKIT
TIMAH

N DAN RD

ROAD
Adam
ROAD

Dover

Botanic
Gardens

HOLLAND

Farrer

COMMONWEALTH

Holland

ROAD

Buona
Vista

Commonwealth

NAPIER RD

Colonial
Residences

ORCHARD ROAD

One-
North

AVENUE

DEMPSEY
HILL

EXPRESSWAY

Queenstown

ALEXANDRA ROAD

NUH

Redhill

Tiong
Bahru

WEST

JALAN BUKIT MERAH

Haw Par
Villa

Telok Blangah
Hill Park

COAST

HIGHWAY

115
Mount Faber

West
Coast

Pasir
Panjang

Alexandra

Telok Blangah

Harbourfront

Harbourfront
Centre

GATEWAY
AVENUE

Pulau
Brani

Sentosa

Pulau
Tekukor

Pulau
Seringat

Pulau
Jong

Pulau Sakijang Bendera
St Johns Island

Pulau
Darat

Pulau Tembakul
Kusu

Pulau Sakijang Pelepah
Lazarus

Pulau
Seking

Pulau
Sebarok

Pulau
Subar Laut

c

d

West Island

Botanic Gardens

HIGHLIGHTS

- Rubber trees
- National Orchid Garden
- Jungle Walk
- Palm Valley
- *Myristica fragans* (nutmeg tree)
- *Cinnamomum zeylanicum* (cinnamon tree)
- Topiary
- Bamboos
- Herbarium

TIP

● Check local papers for details of the free concerts that are held in the Garden's Amphitheater.

Don't leave Singapore without a visit to this 128-acre (52ha) botanical wonder, with its splendid National Orchid Garden. It is best explored in the relative cool of the morning or the evening.

Botanical beginnings Singapore's tranquil botanic gardens are only a few kilometers from frenetic Orchard Road. Thomas Raffles established botanical gardens at the base of Government Hill in 1822, and the collection was moved to its present site in 1859. Over the decades, the gardens have been enlarged and landscaped. The region's first rubber trees, native to Brazil, were propagated here in 1877, and their descendants remain in the gardens. In the 1960s, the gardens supplied many of the seedlings for roadsides and parks all over the island, and the greening of Singapore began.

Clockwise from left: the National Orchid Garden; close-up from the National Orchid Garden; the Ginger Garden; the National Orchid Garden; the entrance gate and the Evolution Garden

Highlights The National Orchid Garden has the largest display of tropical orchids in the world—more than 1,000 species and 2,000 hybrids—with a Cool House for high-altitude orchids and gardens with orchids in natural settings. On the rolling lawn of Palm Valley you'll find "islands" of various palms—more than 115 genera of the major plant group. The nearby patch of tropical rain forest is one of the few remaining areas of Singapore's original vegetation. Australian Black swans and many other water birds live around the Eco-Lake, where there are displays of herbs and spices, medicinal plants, fruit and nut trees, and bamboos. The visitor center has plant displays, water cascades, a café and a great selection of nature books in its excellent shop. The gardens are popular with locals, who jog, picnic and attend the frequent open-air concerts in Palm Valley.

THE BASICS

www.nparks.gov.sg

✚ c3, A4

✉ Junction of Cluny and Holland roads

☎ 6471 7361

🕐 Daily 5am–midnight; National Orchid Garden daily 8.30am–7pm

🍴 Visitor center restaurant and café

🚇 MRT to Orchard, then SBS bus 7, 106, 123 or 174

🚌 As above, plus 75, 105

♿ Good

💰 Botanic Gardens free; admission to Orchid Garden inexpensive

Jurong BirdPark

HIGHLIGHTS

- Penguin feeding time
- Jungle Jewels
- Pelican Cove
- Monorail trip
- Waterfall Aviary
- World of Darkness
- Crowned pigeons
- Birds of paradise
- Southeast Asian hornbills and South American toucans

TIP

● While the monorail may look a bit of a tourist trap, it does provide a good overview of the Park.

Hundreds of penguins and puffins crowded together on an icy beach is an unexpected sight near the equator. And don't miss the Waterfall Aviary, where tropical bird species fly almost free.

The world's birds Jurong BirdPark is Asia-Pacific's biggest bird park—49 acres (20ha)—and home to more than 9,000 birds, many from the tropics. Some 600 species, from all over the world, are housed in aviaries and other apparently open enclosures.

Birds of a feather Not far from the entrance, penguins live in a simulated Antarctic habitat with a swimming area. The vast glass-sided tank has windows 98ft (30m) long. The Waterfall Aviary is the most spectacular area, with 5 acres (2ha) of

Clockwise from left: the Lory Loft; flamingoes in the water; the Birds 'n' Buddies show; feeding time; a parrot and the park monorail

forest contained beneath high netting, with more than 1,500 African birds. The aviary also has a 98ft (30m) man-made waterfall. A monorail gives a good overview of the park, but it's well worth getting off to see the birds close up. The Southeast Asian Birds Aviary re-creates a rain forest, complete with midday storm, and contains more than 260 species, including the colorful parrots. The African Wetlands exhibit, complete with native-style pavilions, includes the Shoebill and African Crown Crane. Jungle Jewels is a large walk-through aviary devoted to hummingbirds and other South American species. The birds of prey and parrots shows are also entertaining. Twice a day the Birds 'n' Buddies show features comedy, audience inter-action and entertaining antics from the park's birds. When you have finished watching birds, cross the road and take a look at the reptile park.

THE BASICS

www.birdpark.com.sg

✚ b3, A7

✉ 2 Jurong Hill

☎ 6265 0022

🕐 Daily 9–6

🍴 Bongo Burgers, Flamingo Café, Ben & Jerry's

🚇 MRT to Boon Lay then SBS bus 194 or 251

♿ Good

💰 Moderate

❓ Bird shows: Birds 'n' Buddies (11, 3), Birds of Prey (10am, 4), Children's Parrot Show (1pm)

Night Safari

HIGHLIGHTS

- "Open" enclosures
- Leopard Trail
- Mouse deer
- Tapirs
- Giraffes
- Lions
- Tigers
- Hippos
- Elephants
- Bats
- Walking trails

TIP

● Check the weather forecast before venturing here, since rain spoils the experience somewhat.

Singapore's Night Safari—a zoo that allows you to see nocturnal animals—is the largest attraction of its kind in the world. Special lights that simulate moonlight illuminate this night zoo.

A world of animals The night safari is divided into eight "geographical" zones that are home to the park's 135 species—more than 900 animals in all. You can expect to see animals from the Southeast Asian rain forests, the African savanna, the Nepalese river valley, the South American pampas and the jungles of Myanmar (Burma). As in the Singapore Zoo, the enclosures are "open" and animals are confined by hidden walls and ditches. Five of these zones have dedicated walking tracks; the others must be visited by tram.

Clockwise from left: close up with the tapirs; the tram is the best way to see the animals; a baby anteater and Chawang, the Asian elephant

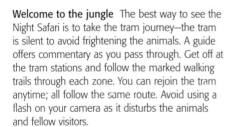

Welcome to the jungle The best way to see the Night Safari is to take the tram journey—the tram is silent to avoid frightening the animals. A guide offers commentary as you pass through. Get off at the tram stations and follow the marked walking trails through each zone. You can rejoin the tram anytime; all follow the same route. Avoid using a flash on your camera as it disturbs the animals and fellow visitors.

What to see Listen for the intermittent roaring of the big cats. The Leopard Trail is one of the busiest walking trails. You can see straight into the enclosure of the prowling leopards—only a plate-glass wall separates you from them. On the Mangrove Walk, fruit bats hang overhead in the gloom, and the elephants, giraffes, tigers and lions are always popular.

THE BASICS

www.nightsafari.com.sg

✚ C2

✉ 80 Mandai Lake Road

☎ 6269 3411

🕐 Daily 7.30pm–midnight

🍴 Ulu Ulu Restaurant

🚇 Ang Mo Kio MRT, then bus 138 or Choa Chu Kang MRT, then bus 927

♿ Reasonable

💰 Expensive

Sentosa

TOP
25

HIGHLIGHTS

- Underwater World
- Images of Singapore
- Cable Car

TIP

- Weekends are busy and atmospheric but to avoid the crowds, visit midweek.

Sentosa is in mid-metamorphisis. The island is now established as a family-friendly leisure park but is discovering a racier side thanks to youth beach culture and a casino development opening 2012.

Fun park Sentosa self-consciously caters to a variety of tastes, so if you're seeking the real Singapore, the island is probably not for you. Land reclamation, beach engineering, and masses of construction have turned this one-time pirates' lair into the closest thing Singapore has to Disneyland. It's still got a lovely green canopy covering, and there are quiet pockets but Sentosa has become mass-market tourist heaven, Starbucks et al.

Rides and thrills New attractions are going up all the time, but highlights include the Underwater

Clockwise from bottom left: residents of Sentosa Butterfly Park; golden statue on Sentosa; Underwater World; jellyfish at Underwater World; tropical marine species at Underwater World; outside the exhibition Images of Singapore

World (which now offers fish reflexology), the Images of Singapore waxwork and diorama exhibition and the kitsch-looking Merlion statue. A new highlight is the USD 22 million Songs of the Sea musical spectacular, an outdoor show than runs twice nightly (7.40 and 8.40). It's aimed at the level of children, but adults may muster some enjoyment from the excellent lighting, pyrotechnics and lasers.

More to do Aside from the plastic attractions, Sentosa is a favourite for families and young people on weekends. There's football and volleyball matches on the beach, and several trendy new bars (Café del Mar and KM8 being the picks), which take Ibiza as their model. Sentosa now has three golf courses, several spas, and resort-style hotels, including one in the luxury Shangri-la chain.

THE BASICS

www.sentosa.com.sg

🞖 c4, A9

✉ Just south of Singapore Island

☎ Sentosa Information Centre 1800 736 8672

🕐 24 hours

🍴 Cafés and restaurants

🚠 Cable car from World Trade Centre (WTC) and Mount Faber

🚌 Harbourfront, then take Sentosa bus

♿ Generally good

💷 Individual venues may charge a cover

Singapore Discovery Centre

The Build It Kids Zone (left); the gateway (middle); the entrance (right) and Little George, the Centre's mascot (opposite)

The Discovery Centre is a world-class "edutainment" attraction that features Singapore's many milestones and achievements in five main galleries.

Visionarium The innovative high-tech exhibits, constructed around eight different themes, present a macro view of the Singapore Story and take you through Singapore's past, present and future, with brilliant light and sound shows and hands-on building activities. One of the highlights is the world's first and largest interactive team-based city design studio, the Visionarium, with a 360-degree screen. During each session, up to 120 guests can design a new city of Singapore and the result is displayed on the huge wraparound screen. A Security Pavilion, with a Crisis Simulation theater, simulates a bomb explosion at an MRT station.

Interactive games The Centre also has several entertaining interactive games and a lively quiz trivia show, located at the Unity Pavilion, and a simulated shooting range, where you can test your eye coordination and shooting skills. Or you can try the even more challenging and exciting Crossfire Paintball. The On Location reporter will take you on a journey through Singapore's history and let you "report" on the nation's milestones.

iWERKS The iWERKS Theatre, next to the main exhibition hall, has a five-story-high screen and state-of-the-art sound system, and offers a truly unforgettable cinematic experience.

Singapore Nature Reserves

HIGHLIGHTS

Bukit Timah
● Macaques
● Strangler figs
● Bird hide

MacRitchie Reservoir Park
● TreeTop Walk
● Birdlife
● Macaques

Sungei Buloh
● Mangrove walkways
● Estuarine crocodiles
● Free guided tours on Saturday

TIP

● The macaques can be a real nuisance here, so resist the temptation to feed them and watch out that they don't snatch food from your hands.

Singapore is renowned for its green open spaces and, given its size, there are a surprising number of reserves where the original vegetation remains.

Bukit Timah The last remaining area of primary tropical rain forest in Singapore covers 410 acres (166ha) of Bukit Timah. Trails that start at the visitor area allow you to observe the reserve's fauna and flora. Lianas and rattans trail and twist through the forest, where you'll see huge strangler figs adorned with bird's nests and staghorn ferns.

MacRitchie Reservoir Park You can jog or walk on the shaded paths around the reservoir's edge; there are exercise stations at intervals. The highlight of several walks through the Park, the TreeTop Walk, is along a freestanding suspension bridge

Bukit Timah Nature Reserve (left); fungi on a tree stump at Bukit Timah Nature Reserve

THE BASICS

www.nparks.gov.sg
Bukit Timah
✚ b2
✉ 177 Hindhede Drive
☎ 6468 5736
🕐 Daily 8.30–6.30
🚇 MRT to Newton, then SBS bus 171 or TIBS 182, 65, 67, 75, 170, 171, 852, 961
♿ None
💵 Free

MacRitchie Reservoir Park
✚ c2
✉ Lornie Road
🕐 24 hours
🍴 Food kiosk
🚇 MRT to Newton, then bus 104, 132 or 167
♿ Good
💵 Free

Sungei Buloh
www.sbwr.org.sg
✚ b1
✉ 301 Neo Tiew Crescent
☎ 6794 1401
🕐 7.30am–7pm Mon–Sat, 7–7 Sun and public hols
🚇 Take SMRT Bus 925 from Kranji MRT Station. Alight at Kranji Reservoir car park and walk for 15 min
♿ Good
💵 Mon–Fri free; Sat, Sun inexpensive

that connects the park's two highest points. From another bridge you can watch tortoises and carp and, if it's switched on, you'll see the fountain, which features 30 water-jet patterns. Concerts take place in the pavilion. Look for the long-tailed macaques, but don't go near them.

Sungei Buloh Singapore's only wetland nature reserve covers 312 acres (130ha). Carefully planned walkways allow you to explore swamp, mangrove and mudflat habitats, and to observe tropical birdlife and many species of marine creatures, particularly mudskippers and crabs. Early morning and evening are the best times for viewing wildlife, with bird life most evident before 10am. From September to March, the reserve is home to migratory birds from as far afield as eastern Siberia.

Singapore Science Centre

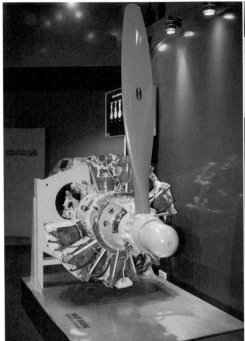

Hundreds of hands-on exhibits excite children and enlighten adults. The world of science and wonder awaits at the Singapore Science Centre, which houses more than 850 exhibits.

Interactive exhibits The Singapore Science Centre attracts more than a million visitors each year. Exhibits in theme galleries offer fascinating insights into human achievements in the physical and life sciences. Many of the exhibits are interactive, and some are supported by talks and films.

Science to hand A laser light display welcomes you in the main lobby. The Aviation Gallery, intro-duces the principles of flight and examines how man first explored the skies. The Life Sciences

Clockwise from left: Singapore Science Centre Aviation Gallery; a giant tongue at the Human Anatomy section; The World of Energy; the human anatomy section; the robotics section and the Atrium laser show

Gallery focuses on the environment and people. You can walk through the internal organs of a human body in the Human Anatomy section. The Discovery Centre aims to stimulate the imagination of younger children with interactive displays, and the Ecogarden is informative for horti-culturalists, with its mini-orchard, hydroponic farm and medicinal garden.

Omni Theatre and Planetarium Next to the Science Centre is the Omni Theatre. This theater has a five-floor high, 75ft (23m) curved Omnimax screen, and state-of-the-art projection and audio equipment with surround sound. You can see films on subjects as diverse as climbing Mt. Everest and the rule of China's first emperors. The features change every six months, so check to find out what's on during your visit.

THE BASICS

www.science.edu.sg

🔠 b3, A7

✉ 15 Science Centre Road

☎ 6425 2500

🕐 SSC Tue–Sun, public hols 10–6. Omni Theatre Tue–Sun, public hols 10–8

🍴 Café in SSC, fast food in Omni Theatre

🚇 Jurong East then 500 yard (500m) walk (turn left from station, along Block 135) or bus 335

🚌 66, 178, 198 direct; 51, 78, 197 to Jurong East Interchange then 335 or walk

🚹 Good

💰 Inexpensive

Singapore Zoo

TOP 25

Treetops Trail, a wooden walkway 20ft (6m) off the ground, lets you join the gibbons and a troop of cheeky red langurs for a monkey's-eye view of a simulated rainforest.

Abandoned pets Singapore's zoo, acclaimed as one of the finest in the world, is also one of the youngest. Its beginnings can be traced back to the 1960s, when British forces pulled out of Singapore and left a ragbag of family pets behind. The zoo, which sprawls over 69 acres (28ha), was officially opened in 1973 and is now home to more than 290 species, some endangered and rare, such as tigers, orangutans, Komodo dragons and golden lion tamarins. Breeding programs have been initiated for endangered species, with some success.

Clockwise from left: kangaroo feeding time; a giraffe; the tiger enclosure is one of the highlights; a young orangutan; feeding time with the orangutans; the zoo entrance and orangutans with orchids

Polar bears and pygmy hippos Living conditions are as near as possible to those in the wild—mini-habitats bounded by naturalistic trenches, moats and rock walls. More than 2,050 animals can be seen. Polar bears, otters and pygmy hippos can be seen close up from underwater viewing areas, and the islands constructed for the different primates provide a clear view of these generally hydrophobic creatures. The snake house is very popular with children and the tiger enclosure is always crowded. There is a great deal to see, and if you get tired of walking, you can always jump onto the silent tram that loops around the fine land-scaped grounds, or take in one of the shows designed to entertain those not content with seeing sea lions, elephants and chimpanzees doing what comes naturally.

THE BASICS

www.zoo.com.sg
✚ c2, D1
✉ 80 Mandai Lake Road
☎ 6269 3411
🕐 Daily 8.30–6
🍴 Restaurants
Ⓜ MRT to Ang Mo Kio then SBS bus 138, or MRT to Choa Chu Kang then TIBS 927
🚌 SBS bus 171 to Mandai Road then cross road and take 138 or 927
♿ Good
💰 Expensive

More to See

CHINESE AND JAPANESE GARDENS

www.jtc.gov.sg

Chinese and Japanese classical gardens have been created on two islands in Jurong Lake. The Chinese Garden covers 32 acres (13ha) and is dotted with pagodas, pavilions and arched bridges. The main building is based on Beijing's Summer Palace. During the mid-autumn festival the gardens are hung with lanterns. The Japanese Gardens are altogether more serene, and take their inspiration from gardens of the 15th to 17th centuries.

✚ b3 ✉ 1 Chinese Garden Road ☎ 6261 3632 🕐 Daily 6am–11pm 🍴 Refreshment kiosks 🚇 Chinese Garden 💵 Inexpensive

COLONIAL RESIDENCES

A walk along Cluny, Lermit and Nassim roads, between the west end of Orchard Road and the Botanic Gardens, will give glimpses of 19th-century colonial residences. These mansions come equiped for making living in the tropical heat as tolerable

as possible: enormous blinds, shaded balconies and verandas, and lush, landscaped gardens.

✚ c3, A3 ✉ Cluny, Lermit and Nassim roads 🚇 Orchard 💵 Free

HARBOURFRONT

The Harbourfront Precinct, which includes the Singapore Cruise Centre, spans 59 acres (24ha) along Singapore's southern waterfront at the foothills of Mount Faber, and over-looks the resort island of Sentosa (▷ 62). A popular destination, this former exhibition area has been transformed into a waterfront hub for work, living and recreation, as well as a great waterfront dining destination. Be sure to check out VivoCity (▷ 47), Singapore's largest shopping mall, and the city's latest entertainment area, St. James Power Station.

✚ B9, c4 ✉ 1 Maritime Square 🕐 7am–midnight daily 🚇 Harbourfront

HAW PAR VILLA (TIGER BALM GARDENS)

This theme park, built in 1937, is

Brightly painted statue at Haw Par Villa

Bonsai Garden at the Chinese Gardens

based on Chinese myth and legend and real crimes in old Singapore. Brightly painted statues, boat rides, a 197ft (60m) long dragon and animated puppets will entertain children. 🔲 c3 ✉ 262 Pasir Panjang Road ☎ 6872 2780 🕐 Daily 9–7 🍴 Cafés 🚇 MRT Buona Vista then bus 200 💷 Free

KRANJI WAR MEMORIAL

The War Memorial is dedicated to the service personnel from Malaya, India, Sri Lanka, Australia, New Zealand, Britain and Canada who died defending Singapore and Malaya against the Japanese during World War II. More than 4,000 graves stand in rows along the well-kept lawns, and the names of those whose bodies were not recovered (more than 24,000) are inscribed on the sides of the memorial's 12 walls. The cemetery, a hospital burial ground during the occupation, became a military cemetery after the war.
🔲 b1 ✉ 9 Woodlands Road 🕐 Daily 7am–6pm 🚌 SBS bus 170 from Rochor Road 🚇 Kranji Station 💷 Free

MANDAI ORCHID GARDENS
www.mandai.com.sg

Many of the orchid hybrids on display at these gardens are stunning, especially the Vanda "Mandai Glow", with its beautiful blend of peach and pale orange.

Orchids have been grown on this site since 1951, when the land was leased by a couple of enthusiasts, John Laycock and Lee Kim Hong. It wasn't until 1956 that the gardens were turned into a commercial venture. Following Laycock's death, Amy Ede, his adopted daughter, managed the gardens. The area under cultivation has increased over the years to 10 acres (4ha) and today the orchid gardens are the largest on the island. Millions of sprays are exported all over the world each year, kept in good condition using a unique technology developed by the owners.

The gardens are packed with gorgeous blooms, some native, some introduced, as well as the many hybrids that have been the making of the Singapore orchid industry.

Kranji War Memorial Cemetery

A pink orchid in the Mandai Orchid Gardens

Amazingly, despite the vast array of species on display, all orchids have the same shape—three sepals and three petals, but one of the petals, known as the "lip," is a different shape from the others.

The deep pink and white flowers of Vanda "Miss Joaquim," Singapore's national flower, can be seen in abundance, as can many other varieties, including delicate slipper orchids and fantastic moth orchids. An hour's stroll in the gardens, which also contain a landscaped water garden, makes a gentle start to the day. The Singapore Zoo and Night Safari are close by.
✚ C2 ✉ 200 Mandai Lake Road ☎ 6269 1036 🕐 Mon 8–6, Tue–Sun 8–7 🚇 MRT to Ang Mo Kio then SBS bus 138 🚌 SBS bus 171 to Mandai Road, then cross road for 138, or TIBS 927 ♿ None 💰 Inexpensive
❓ Boxed orchids can be sent abroad—details in shop

MEMORIES AT OLD FORD FACTORY

www.s1942.org.sg
It was at this building, on 15 February 1942, Lt.-Gen. A. E. Percival, Commander of the British Forces in Singapore, surrendered to the Japanese Army.

Soon after, Singapore was renamed Syonan-To (Light of the South) and for nearly four years the Japanese ruled Singapore. The art deco-style building, originally built as Ford's first assembly plant in Asia, is now refurbished as a gallery showing the exhibition "Syonan Years: Singapore Under Japanese Rule, 1942–1945."

The exhibition, curated by the National Archives of Singapore, provides the background of World War II in Malaya and describes the hardships people endured during the Occupation. The pathway leading to the building was the ceremonial route taken by the British forces on the day of the surrender, and you enter the exhibition gallery through a tunnel, starting at the historic Board Room, where the signing of the surrender took place. On display are archival photographs, oral history interviews, maps and artefacts from the era.

Memories at Old Ford Factory

"He Ping"–Peace On the mezzanine floor is an AV cinema showing documentaries on various aspects of the Japanese Occupation and featuring exclusive footage from the depths of the archives. In the grounds of the museum is a granite stone inscribed with a Tang dynasty verse entitled "Taking History as a Lesson" and a calligraphic sculpture entitled "He Ping" or Peace, which signifies the relief and calm that comes at the end of war. Behind the old main wing is a garden plot with wartime crops, such as sugar cane and oil palm.

➕ b2 ✉ 351 Upper Bukit Timah Road ☎ 6332 7973 🕐 Mon–Fri 9–5.30; Sat, 9–1.30. Closed on Sun and public holidays 🚇 MRT to Clementi then SBS 184 🚌 SBS Bus 170 ♿ Reasonable 💰 Inexpensive

NUS CENTRE FOR THE ARTS

www.nus.edu.sg/museum
The centre manages Singapore National University's three art collections. The Chinese art collection, located at lobby level in the Lee Kong Chian Art Museum, has six galleries of paintings, calligraphy, ceramics and bronze objects representing every major era of China's long and illustrious history.

The South and Southeast Asian collection, at concourse level in the South and Southeast Asian Gallery, displays artworks that span classical to modern traditions in drawing and painting, textile, ceramics, sculptures and bronzes from around the region. Some of the works display historic traditions but there's plenty to keep fans of modern Asian art happy, including contemporary paintings, and textiles acquired during recent field trips.

The Ng Eng Teng collection, at the top level in the Ng Eng Teng Gallery, contains more than 1,000 items— sculptures, vessels, ceramic forms, paintings and drawings—by Singapore's foremost sculptor.

➕ b3 ✉ University Cultural Centre Annex, 50 Kent Ridge Crescent, National University of Singapore ☎ 6516 4617 🕐 Mon–Sat 10–5 🚌 MRT to Clementi Station, then bus number 96 💰 Free

Exhibits in the NUS Centre for the Arts

Porcelain Buddha gilt-bronze mask, NUS Centre for the Arts

A Walk through the Botanic Gardens

This walk takes you through the National Orchid Garden (▷ 56–57), so a good time to start is around opening hour—8.30am.

DISTANCE: 1–1.5 miles (1.5–2.5km) **ALLOW:** 2–3 hours

▷ 56–57

START

TANGLIN GATE (MAIN GATE)
✚ A3, A4, c3 🚇 MRT to Orchard, then SBS Bus 7, 106, 123, 174

END

TANGLIN GATE OR VISITOR CENTRE

WALK

WEST ISLAND

❶ Take the path to the left that leads to the March Garden ponds. These lovely ponds, created out of a natural wetlands, feature local and non-native water plants.

❷ Keep walking to the left around the ponds and follow some stepping stones. Take the turn to the right and walk along to Swan Lake, with its resident white swans and exuberant "Swing Me Mama" sculpture.

❸ Continue walking straight ahead until several paths meet and you can see three sets of steps. Take the middle steps to the Sundial Garden—you'll see a Floral Clock on the far side.

❹ Climb the steps to the left of the Floral Clock and turn left. Keep going and you'll reach the Sun Rockery, and a little farther on there is a display of the gorgeous Vanda "Miss Joaquim" orchid, the national flower of Singapore.

❽ Walk downhill to leave the Orchid Gardens. Stroll down the lawn at Palm Valley and admire the palms, then relax by Symphony Lake, before walking up to the Visitor Centre.

❼ Down the hill to the right you'll find a huge collection of bromeliads, and the Cool House nearby that houses tropical montane orchid species. From here you loop back up to the Orchidarium, with its lowland species.

❻ A path from the Ginger Garden will take you directly to the Orchid Plaza and National Orchid Garden. Turn right once you're inside the gardens and walk to the fountain. Turn left here and walk uphill to the Tan Hoon Siang Mist House.

❺ When you reach the end of the orchid display, you'll see an extremely tall forest tree—walk down the path at its side and along to the Ginger Garden, home to plants in the ginger family and related species.

Shopping

ANTIQUES OF THE ORIENT
www.aoto.com.sg
You could spend hours browsing through this shop's fine selection of old lithographs, prints, maps and books.
⊞ B4 ✉ 01–48/49 Tanglin Shopping Centre, 19 Tanglin Road ☎ 6734 9351
Ⓗ Mon–Sat 10.30–6.30, Sun 10.30–4.30 Ⓜ Orchard

BURMESE FINE ARTS
Specializes in Cambodian, Burmese and Thai objects and curios. The reputable dealer offers certificates of authenticity.
⊞ A4 ✉ 03–10 Holland V Shopping Centre, Holland Village ☎ 6466 9089 Ⓗ Mon–Sat 10–6 ☒ 7, 61, 106

HOLLAND ROAD SHOPPING CENTRE
Ethnic goods from all over Asia. Includes porcelain, cloisonné, arts and crafts and clothing.
⊞ A4 ✉ 211 Holland Avenue ☎ 6338 8135 Ⓗ Daily 10–9 ☒ 5, 7, 61, 10 Ⓠ MRT Buona Vista then bus 200

LIM'S ARTS & CRAFTS
Authentic handicrafts, including linens, jewelry, pottery and silk pyjamas.
⊞ A4 ✉ 02–01 Holland Road Shopping Centre, 211 Holland Avenue ☎ 6467 1300
Ⓗ Mon–Sat 9.30–8.30, Sun, public holidays 10.30–6.30
☒ 5, 7, 61, 106

MATA HARI ANTIQUES
The basketry, lacquerware

and silver jewelry here originate from Thailand, Cambodia, Vietnam, Indonesia and Myanmar (Burma).
⊞ B4 ✉ 02–26 Tanglin Shopping Centre, 19 Tanglin Road ☎ 6737 6068
Ⓗ Mon–Sat 10.30–6.30 Ⓜ Orchard

SELECT BOOKS
This cozy bookshop carries Singapore's largest selection of books on Southeast Asia, with an extensive range of academic texts, travel guides and coffee-table books.
⊞ B4 ✉ 03–15 Tanglin Shopping Centre, 19 Tanglin Road ☎ 6732 1515
Ⓗ Mon–Sat 9.30–6.30 , Sun 10–4.30 Ⓜ Orchard

CARPET AUCTIONS
Taking in a carpet auction can be a fun way to spend a Sunday. Several carpet companies hold auctions then, usually at the Hyatt, the Hilton or the Holiday Inn. Carpets are spread out for easy viewing from about 10 until just after noon. Estimated market prices are posted and a Continental-type buffet breakfast is often free to participants. Auctions usually start about 1. Depending on the number of viewers and the size of their wallets, bidding proceeds at a fast pace. Expect to get 50–70 percent off the estimated price, or at least start the bidding there.

TANGLIN MALL
www.tanglinmall.com.sg
This shopping mall provides something a little different from the designer labels on offer elsewhere on Orchard Road. The range of stores includes some interesting children's shops, a sports shop and three floors of Food Junction. A handicrafts market is held the third Saturday of every month.
⊞ B4 ✉ 163 Tanglin Road ☎ 6736 4922 Ⓗ Daily 10–9 Ⓜ Orchard

TANGLIN SHOPPING CENTRE
www.tanglinsc.com
One of the area's oldest shopping malls, this is known for Asian antiques and curios (though, as elsewhere in Singapore, prices are high). It is also good for carpets, tailoring and cameras and accessories. Near the intersection of Tanglin and Orchard roads.
⊞ B4 ✉ 19 Tanglin Road ☎ 6737 0849 Ⓗ Mon–Sat 10.30–6.30 Ⓜ Orchard

TERESE JADE & MINERALS
Jade is a Chinese favorite. Check out the loose beads and stones—you can make your own jewelry or have it custom made on the premises.
⊞ B4 ✉ 01–28 Tanglin Shopping Centre, 19 Tanglin Road ☎ 6734 0379
Ⓗ Mon–Sat 10.30–6.30 Ⓜ Orchard

WEST ISLAND

SHOPPING

Restaurants

PRICES

Prices are approximate, based on a 3-course meal for one person.
$$$ over S$50
$$ S$20–S$50
$ under S$20

COFFEE CLUB, HOLLAND VILLAGE ($)

The Coffee Club specializes in interesting coffees, some with cream and a choice of different spirits. There is also a selection of pastas, salads and sandwiches.
🕂 A4 ✉ 48 Lorong Mambong ☎ 6466 0296 🕐 Sun–Thu 11am–midnight, Fri–Sat 11am–1am 🚌 5, 7, 61, 106

LA FORKETTA ($$$)

Although this Italian restaurant is a little off the beaten track it's worth the trip, as the food is delicious, particularly the first-class pizza.
🕂 D5 ✉ 491 River Valley Road ☎ 6836 3373 🕐 Daily 12–3, 6–10.30 🚌 14, 32, 54, 65, 139, 195

AL FORNO TRATTORIA ($$$)

A popular restaurant, though a little way out of the heart of the city, so be sure to make a reservation. Antipasto and pizzas are particularly tasty.
🕂 D2 ✉ 203 Thomson Road ☎ 6256 2838 🕐 Tue–Sun 12–2, 6.30–10.30 🚇 Novena

MICHELANGELO'S ($$)

Innovative Italian cuisine from this multi-award-winning restaurant comes in generous portions served by professional staff. Dine among the fresco paintings or eat outside by candlelight.
🕂 A4 ✉ 01–60 Chip Bee Gardens, Block 44 Jalan Merah Saga ☎ 6475 9069 🕐 Mon–Sun 11.30–2.30, 6.30–10.30 🚌 7, 61, 106

ORIGINAL SIN ($$)

The menu at this Mediterranean-style restaurant is completely vegetarian. The imagina-

COFFEE SHOPS

Singapore's traditional coffee shops are nothing like the modern places that sell a sophisticated selection of Javanese coffee and brownies. They are no-nonsense, cheap and cheerful options for popular local rice and noodle dishes. You also get coffee, but it's thick and sweet, made with condensed milk. Mindful of waste, coffee shops sometimes serve take-out coffee in empty condensed-milk cans, and you will occasionally see people carrying these, though the more usual coffee container today is the familiar Styrofoam container or a plastic bag, which you can sometimes see tied to railings while the contents cool.

tive use of ingredients gives run-of-the-mill dishes a real twist.
🕂 Off map to west ✉ 01–62 Chip Bee Gardens, Block 43, Jalan Merah Saga, Holland Village ☎ 6475 5605 🕐 Tue–Sun 11–2.30, 6–10.30 🚌 5, 7, 61, 106

ROCHESTER PARK ($$$)

This trendy new dining district, close to Holland Village, has four smart restaurants in colonial bungalows. Choices are Chinese, Continental, Italian and Tex-Mex. Expensive, quality food.
🕂 A4 ✉ Rochester Park 🚇 Buena Vista

ROCKY'S ($$)

If you feel like ordering pizza to eat in, Rocky's is the place. You need to allow about an hour for delivery.
🕂 Off map to north ✉ Block 106, 12 Clementi Street ☎ 6468 9188 🕐 Daily 11–10.30 (last order 10) 🚇 No public transport

SAMY'S CURRY ($)

Located in a former civil-service clubhouse, with a colonial edifice and overhead fans; meals here are served on banana leaves. Try spoonfuls of zesty curries, fragrant rices, breads and assorted condiments.
🕂 A4 ✉ Singapore Civil Service Club House, Block 25, Dempsey Road ☎ 6472 2080 🕐 Daily 11–3, 6–10 🚇 Orchard

The east of Singapore boasts long, sandy beaches lined with excellent seafood restaurants, recreational water sports, including a cable ski park, poignant World War II memorials and historical temples.

Sights	82–87	Top 25	**25**
Walk	88	Changi Chapel and Museum ▷ **82**	
Shopping	90	Joo Chiat Road ▷ **83**	
		East Coast Park ▷ **84**	
Entertainment and Nightlife	91		
Restaurants	92		

MAL

Pulau
Punggol Timor

Pulau
Serangoon

Mamam Beach

Pulau
Tekong

Pulau Ubin
Beach

PUNGGOL

Punggol

EXPRESSWAY

PUNGGOL ROAD

ngkang

SENGKANG

Buangkok

HOUGANG

Hougang

TAMPINES

AIRPORT ROAD

BARTLEY ROAD

Upper Pays
Lebar

Macpherson

Eunos

MALAY
VILLAGE

aya

Dakota

o Chiat
Road

Crocodile
Farm

Coney Island
Beach

Pulau
Ketam

Pulau Ubin

Pulau Ubin
Ferry Terminal

Pulau Ubin
Park

Changi
Beach

PASIR RIS

Pasir Ris
Beach

Serangoon
Harbour

Pasir Ris
Park

TAMPINES

Pasir Ris

EXPRESSWAY

Escape Theme
Park

Changi
Village

CHANGI

LOYANG AVENUE

TAMPINES AVENUE 10

Tampines

Bedok
Reservoir

PAN-ISLAND

EXPRESSWAY

SIMEI

Simei

SIMEI AVE.

CHANGI ROAD

Changi
International
Airport

Changi Ferry
Terminal

AIRPORT ROAD

Changi
Airport

Changi
Chapel &
Museum

Expo

XILIN AVENUE

AIRPORT BOULEVARD

CHANGI COAST ROAD

CHANGI
EAST

Kembangan NEW UPPER

Bedok

BEDOK

EAST

COAST

COAST

EAST

ROAD

PARKWAY

Tanah
Merah

Newater
Visitor
Centre

Safra
Golf Course

National
Sailing Centre

CHANGI ROAD

Tanah Merah
Ferry Terminal

Spark Sea
Adventure Park

East Coast Beach

Bedok
Jetty

Marine Cove

East Coast
Park

Republic of Singapore
Air Force Museum

0   5 km
0   3 miles

d   e

East Island

Changi Chapel and Museum

The Changi Chapel (left) and the museum chapel memorial wall (right)

THE BASICS

www.changimuseum.com

🚌 e2

✉ 1000 Upper Changi Road North

☎ 6214 2451

🕐 Daily 9.30–5

🚇 Tanah Merah. Take SBS bus 2 from station

♿ Free

HIGHLIGHTS

- Replica Murals
- Video screenings
- Wartime plants

During World War II, some 50,000 civilians, Allied troops and prisoners were incarcerated in Singapore. Exhibits at the Changi Prison Chapel and Museum portray the terrible conditions they endured—some for more than three years.

Fitting memorial Housed within the open-air courtyard of the museum, the Changi Chapel is a reconstruction of one of the many chapels built at Changi Prison during the Japanese Occupation. This poignant monument to those who strived to maintain their faith during their years in captivity is a fitting memorial to all who were imprisoned.

Changi Murals The museum displays photographs, letters, drawings and personal effects of some of the tens of thousands of civilians, soldiers and other war prisoners. There is also a replica of the original Changi Murals, which were painted by bombardier Stanley Warren. Visitors are welcome to join the 9am Sunday services, conducted by various church groups at the Changi Chapel.

"Elizabeth Choy" There are regular screenings of videos such as "Changi Through The Eyes of Haxworth" about a prisoner whose sketches vividly capture his years in Changi, and "Elizabeth Choy," the story of a civilian heroine who withstood nearly 200 days of imprisonment and torture. Tours are available from 10am, with the last tour at 3.45pm. There is a café and the garden has a collection of plants that Singapore residents typically planted during the Japanese Occupation.

Wonderful original architecture and intriguing old businesses by day, and an exciting mix of restaurants and music lounges in the evening, give a fascinating glimpse of former times and a sample of Singapore life today.

History This once quiet seaside village is today an eclectic mix of colonial villas, Peranakan-style terraces and Malay bungalows. Some are pre-served, many are being renovated, others remain untouched. The Joo Chiat Complex, at the north-ern end of Joo Chiat near the Malay Village, is a busy local shopping complex selling fabrics and household goods at bargain prices. Next to the Village is the Geylang Serai market (▷ 90), a traditional Asian market, a good place to browse.

Eclectic mix Opposite Guan Hoe Soon Restaurant (which serves traditional Peranakan nonya dishes) is a typical 1920s corner terrace, with an ornate frieze of green dragons on the roof pediment. Terrace houses with covered walkways can be found along the road. The second floors may be pillared verandas (No. 113), or have ornate case-ment windows (Nos. 370–76). Colorful tiles are a common feature (Nos. 137–39). Koon Seng Road, to the left, has two rows of terrace houses with courtyard gardens in front and extravagant moldings, tiles and paintwork. Set in dense gar-dens are Malay-style bungalows (Nos. 229, 382) fronted by verandas flanked by staircases. Villas to the southern end (Nos. 507–509) indicate that this was the seafront before land reclamation.

THE BASICS

➕ d3
✉ Joo Chiat Road
☎ Guan Hoe Soon 6344 2761. Katong Antique House 6345 8544
🍴 Guan Hoe Soon (nonya food, No. 214); Casa Bom Vento (No. 47); Mum's Kitchen (No. 314); AJ Tandoori's (No. 328); Lemongrass (✉ 899 East Coast Road)
Ⓜ Paya Lebar then walk
🚌 16, 33
♿ None
🖐 Free

HIGHLIGHTS

● Guan Hoe Soon Restaurant
● Joo Chiat Complex
● Katong Antique House
● Koon Seng Road
● Malay Village
● Malay-style bungalows
● Old seafront luxury villas
● Peranakan-style shophouses
● Residential terraces

East Coast Park

HIGHLIGHTS

- Big Splash water rides
- Canoe rental
- East Coast Sailing Centre
- Parkland Golf Driving Range
- Tennis center
- SKI360

TIP

- Singapore's freshest seafood can be found at many of the waterfront eateries, but avoid Sunday, when they are always packed.

Two decades of land reclamation have created this beachside playground. Swim or sail; walk, jog or cycle the 6 miles (10km) of tracks between coconut groves; or laze on white sands.

Plenty to do Picnicking families flock to the area on the weekends. There are many places to rent a bicycle, canoe, Rollerblades or a deck chair, and it's a pleasant place to relax and catch a cooling breeze in the evening. The East Coast Seafood Centre is popular with those who appreciate excellent seafood, but it is only open in the evening and loses some of the beach ambience amid a large concrete plaza. The East Coast Lagoon Food Village farther east is another popular spot, and feels slightly more down to earth and natural.

Clockwise from left: a beach scene at East Coast Park; a lone bicycle on the beach; enjoying a picnic bbq; the cable ski park; you can also rent bicycles here

East Coast Sailing Centre Sailboards and laser dinghies can be rented here. If you encounter difficulties at sea, a rescue boat is on hand to bring you back to the East Coast Sailing Centre.

Marina Cove Next to the park at Marina Cove are clay tennis courts (open until late evening), a cable ski park (SKI360°), where an overhead cable pulls you across the water at speeds of up to 37mph (60km/h). Golfers can practice at the two-tier, 163-yard (150m) Parkland for just the cost of the balls. You can also rent bicycles, Rollerblades and canoes. At the Big Splash, water rides delight adults and children alike.

Beaches The 12 miles (20km) of beaches are popular on weekends, but swimming in the often murky waters is not advised.

THE BASICS

www.nparks.gov.sg

🚹 d3, L5, M5

✉ East Coast Service Road

☎ ECSC 6449 5118. Tennis Centre 6243 1792. Parkland Golf Range 6440 6726. Big Splash 6345 1321. SKI360° 6442 7318

🍴 East Coast Lagoon Food Centre and Jumbo Seafood (▷ 92), various kiosks, fast food at Marina Cove and Big Splash

🚇 Bedok then bus 401 or bus 31, 197; Eunos then 55, 155; Paya Lebar then 76, 135 and walk

🚌 16, 31, 55, 76, 135, 155, 196, 197, 853 daily to Marine Parade Road; 401 to East Coast Service Road (Sun)

♿ Some level paths

💲 Free; rental charges per hour for sports, etc

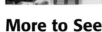

More to See

BISHAN HDB ESTATE

More than 84 percent of Singapore's population lives in state-subsidized Housing and Development Board apartments (HDBs). Hundreds of these government-built blocks exist in any given area, each a small town in its own right. Bishan was developed in the early 1990s. As with most HDB areas, it has its own MRT station, around which a shopping and entertainment complex, Junction 8, has been built. Wander around Junction 8's central area, up Bishan Road, and from there turn right in front of the MRT, then left into Street 22. You'll come upon one of the many smaller satellite areas, complete with its own shops and hawker center at the base of the housing blocks. On the outskirts of Bishan, at Bright Hill Drive, is Phor Kark See, a huge Buddhist temple overlooking Bishan Park.

✚ c2 ✉ Bishan Central 🍴 3rd Mini Steamboat Delight, 9 Bishan Place, 04–01G and numerous other coffee shops, hawker centers and fast-food outlets 🚇 Bishan 🚌 13, 53, 54, 55, 56, 156 ♿ Few 👊 Free

MALAY VILLAGE

The Malays, the native inhabitants of Singapore, were dispersed by the British from the mouth of the Singapore River in the 1840s and moved to the area now known as Geylang. Descendants of that community, along with a large population of Indonesians, now live there. Geylang is a fascinating area, especially during Muslim religious holidays. The Malay Village complex features aspects of Malay culture and history, while the nearby Geylang Serai Market (▷ 90) is crammed with stalls, and right at the end is a hawker food center. The wet market is incredible! You can visit a traditional kampong to see how the Malays lived in the 1950s and 1960s, and try traditional crafts and games.

✚ d3 ✉ 39 Geylang Serai ☎ 6748 4700 🕐 Daily 10–10 🚇 Paya Lebar 👊 Free to village; Kampung Days and Cultural Museum, adults S$5, children S$3

PASIR RIS PARK

This 175-acre (71ha) area contains some of Singapore's last remaining

Bishan HDB Estate

stretches of mangrove swamp, and is now a bird and nature reserve. Raised boardwalks meander through this habitat. Look for fiddler crabs, mudskippers and small-clawed otters. Birds you might spot include herons, yellow-vented bulbuls, brown-throated sunbirds and collared kingfishers.

🏛 e2 ✉ Off Jalan Loyang Kecil 🕐 24 hours 🚇 MRT to Pasir Ris then bus 403 🖐 Free

REPUBLIC OF SINGAPORE AIR FORCE MUSEUM

www.mindef.gov.sg/rsaf/about/te-afm.asp
This museum allows close-up inspection of a wide range of aircraft, from an early Cessna to the more recent A4-S Skyhawk. On the first level, the museum has a "History of Aviation" exhibition, while upstairs are eight indoor galleries where you'll learn about the history of the RSAF, see models of past and present aircraft, radar and weapons systems, and an interactive model of the Tengah Air Base. Gallery 4 features a Bloodhound missile and an interactive model of the Launch Control Post. Would-be pilots will enjoy the Flight Simulator in Gallery 5. The presentation is highly interactive, with multimedia displays.

🏛 d3 ✉ 400 Airport Road ☎ 6461 8504/8506 🕐 Tue–Sun 8.30–5 🍴 Cafeteria 🚌 SBS 90 and 94 (SBS 90 not available on Sun) 🖐 Free

SIONG LIM TEMPLE

Set amid HDB residential towers, the Siong Lim Temple is a national monument to Singapore's Chinese immigrants, built between 1868 and 1908. The architecture incorporates elements of the building styles of Fujian province, in southeast China, from where the original laborers came from. The seven-floor gold-topped pagoda is a replica of the one at the 800-year-old Shanfeng temple in Fujian. The oldest building, a small wooden shrine, contains murals of the much-loved Chinese legend "Journey to the West."

🏛 d3 ✉ 184E Jalan Toa Payoh ☎ 6259 6924 🕐 Daily 6.30am–9pm 🚇 A short walk from Toa Payoh MRT Station 🖐 Free

Pasir Ris Park mangrove boardwalk

Pony rides at Pasir Ris Park

East Coast Park Walk

This recreational park (▷ 84–85) running for 12 miles (20km) along the East Coast, has water sports and seafood restaurants.

DISTANCE: 1–1.5 miles (1.5–2.5km) **ALLOW:** 2–3 hours

START

END

BUS STOP
✚ e3 🚌 Bedok then 401, or 31, 197; Eunos then 55, 155, 196 to Marine Crescent and Marine Terrace

BUS STOP

1 Walk to the lagoon, where you can watch cable-skiers of all ages practice their wakeboarding skills at SKI360°. Bring your bathing suit and have a go!

6 Take a walk farther down the beach or a quiet nap under a beach-side coconut tree before you return to the bus stop for the trip back to the Bedok Interchange.

2 When you're finished, head north up the beach to the East Coast Lagoon Food Centre, a popular hawker area, for a cool, fresh tropical fruit drink and an exotic snack.

5 By now you should have worked up a real appetite, so head south down the beach to the East Coast Seafood Centre, where there are eight restaurants specializing in seafood. Try the local favorites—crispy baby octopus, drunken prawns and chilli crab—wonderful!

3 Continue on up the beach to the nearby Pasta Fresca Sea Sports Centre and rent a sailboat or a sailboard or just sit in the shade and watch the action.

4 If there's not much wind, you can rent a dinghy a bit farther up the beach and row to the nearby Bedok Jetty, which is popular with recreational fisherfolk.

Shopping

APOLLO GOLDSMITHS

One of many shops that sells gold jewelry along Buffalo Road and Serangoon Road. Gold is sold by the gram, so any difference in cost is due to the design and work.
🕂 F5 ✉ 01–08, Blk 664 Buffalo Road ☎ 6296 1838 🕐 Mon–Sat 10.30–8.30, Sun 10–6 🚇 Bugis

BATIK EMPORIUM

Leather, briefcases, camera cases and purses, as well as batik shirts, dresses and sarongs.
🕂 F4 ✉ 138 Arab Street ☎ 6294 7559 🕐 Mon–Sat 10–7.30, Sun 12–6.30 🚇 Bugis

BUGIS JUNCTION

www.bugisjunction-mall.com.sg
An interesting glass-covered shopping street with shophouses, modern retail outlets, a movie theater, and the Japanese department store, Seiyu.
🕂 F5 ✉ 200 Bugis Junction 🕐 6557 6557 🚇 Bugis

BUGIS STREET

The simple clothes, accessory and shoe stalls in the largest street shopping venue in Singapore attracts hordes of bargain hunters. You can also pick up a fresh fruit juice or enjoy cheap fish.
🕂 F5 ✉ Off Victoria Street, near Rocher Road ☎ 6338 9513 🕐 Daily 2pm–10pm 🚇 Bugis

CHANGI VILLAGE

Specialty shops in a village atmosphere. Everything at bargain prices: electronic equipment, shoes, batik dresses, Indian cotton clothing, kimonos, and carpets.
🕂 e2 ✉ North of Changi Airport 🚇 Tanah Merah, then take SBS bus no.2

GEYLANG SERAI

Located in Geylang, this is the cultural heart of the Malay community in Singapore. The buildings house restaurants and shops specializing in traditional Malay cuisine and crafts. The two paid-for attractions Kampung Days and the Cultural Museum are in the Malay Village (▷ 86) and levy a fee. But the area is free to wander around.
🕂 d3 ✉ Geylang Serai

ANTIQUES

Furniture and objects more than 100 years old, considered antiques, are sold in a plethora of antiques and reproduction shops. Buy only from reputable dealers. They will give a certificate of antiquity or a detailed description along with a receipt. This proof may be required to ensure duty-free importation to the US and UK. Prices are usually lower in the country of origin than in Singapore; they vary widely here, and bargaining is essential.

☎ 6294 7559 🕐 Daily 10–10 🚇 Paya Lebar

POPPY FABRIC

All the colors of the rainbow are represented in the lovely Thai and Chinese silks in this store and in other stores specializing in textiles along Arab Street.
🕂 F4 ✉ 111 Arab Street ☎ 6296 6352 🕐 Mon–Sat 10–6.15 🚇 Bugis

SIM LIM SQUARE

Several floors of shops sell electronic goods, including appliances, computers, software and televisions. Look for the red star that indicates a "Good Retailer" approved by the STB (▷ 11).
🕂 F5 ✉ 1 Rochor Canal Road ☎ 6336 3922 🕐 Mon–Sat 11–8, Sun 11–7 (shops' hours may vary) 🚇 Bugis

THANDAPANI CO

This traditional provisions shop specializes in spices used in Indian cooking.
🕂 F5 ✉ 124 Dunlop Street ☎ 6292 3163 🕐 Daily 9–9 🚇 Bugis

CENTURY SQUARE AND TAMPINES MALL

These malls are hugely popular with Tampines residents and convenient for a last-minute splurge before leaving from Changi Airport.
🕂 e2 ✉ 2-4 Tampines Central ☎ 6789 6261; 6788 8370 🚇 MRT: Tampines

Entertainment and Nightlife

CHANGI SAILING CLUB

Although a private club and a long way out of town, this makes a lovely, relaxing place for an evening drink and meal, which can be taken on the small balcony overlooking the beach, under the palm trees or in the comfortable bar. Nonmembers are admitted for a dollar Monday to Friday evenings.

➕ e3 ✉ 32 Netheravon Road ☎ 6545 2876 🕐 Restaurant: daily 10–10 🚇 MRT to Tampines then bus 29

DOWNTOWN EAST

www.downtowneast.com.sg
This giant theme park-cum-resort has lots of entertainment choices at affordable prices: food courts, retail shopping, gaming areas and a children's play area.

➕ e2 ✉ Pasir Ris Drive 3, next to Pasir Ris Park ☎ 6589 1688 🕐 Daily 9am until late 🚇 Pasir Ris, then take Shuttle Bus

DXO

www.dxo.com.sg
Offers martinis and champagne and an outdoor view of the Marina Promenade from the Nest, where you can chill out and enjoy Retro, R&B and the commercial Top 40s.

➕ F6 ✉ 8 Raffles Avenue, Esplanade Mall 🕐 Daily 5pm until late ☎ 6582 4896 🚇 Millenia

INDIAN DANCE

www.nas.org.sg
Singapore's Indian population takes its dance very seriously, and local dance academies put on public performances. The exacting steps and hand gestures, the exciting rhythms and the brilliant costumes of dance forms such as *orissi* are an unusual delight and well worth checking out.

Nrityalaya Aesthetics Society
➕ F5 ✉ Stamford Arts Centre, 155 Waterloo Street ☎ 6336 6537 🚇 Bugis

JOO CHIAT ROAD

The southerly section of this famous old strip is a fabulous place to sample the laid-back and casual side to Singapore nightlife, from cold beers fold-away pavement tables to karaoke and girlie bars. It's sleazy in parts, but safe and a refreshing change from the super trendy downtown establishments.

DANCE CLUBS

Like elsewhere, Singapore dance clubs tend to suit particular groups of revelers. While expats can be found at such places as Harry's Quayside and Papa Joe's, the mostly young locals find Ministry of Sound (▷ 48) and Zouk (▷ 49) suit their tastes . Cover charges range from S$12 to S$25 and usually include one drink.

Head for the junction with East Coast Road.

➕ d3 ✉ Joo Chiat Road, junction with East Coast Road 🕐 Daily from dusk 🚇 MRT: Paya Labar (then walk or take a taxi)

KALLANG NETBALL CENTRE

This modern facility is within the same precinct as the National Stadium. There are six courts here but you should call ahead.

➕ J4, d3 ✉ 52 Stadium Blvd ☎ 6348 1291 🕐 Daily 7am–10pm 🚇 Kallang

SINGAPORE INDOOR STADIUM

www.sis.gov.sg
This US$65 million stadium is the home of big sporting and live music events in Singapore. The ultramodern design includes a giant roof that resembles the Chinese character for the "lucky" number eight. Elton John, the Rolling Stones and the Harlem Globetrotters are among those who have played here.

➕ d3 ✉ Stadium Walk ☎ 6344 2660 🕐 Check events 🚌 11, 16, 608

TAMPINES STADIUM ROCK CLIMBING WALL

This excellent wall is one of the many in Singapore.
➕ d2 ✉ 25 Tampines Street ☎ 6781 1980 🕐 Daily 9am–11pm 🚇 Tampines

Restaurants

PRICES

Prices are approximate, based on a 3-course meal for one person.

$$$ over S$50
$$ S$20–S$50
$ under S$20

BANANA LEAF APOLLO ($$)

A southern Indian "banana-leaf" restaurant where the leaf takes the place of a plate—with a good range of dishes to accompany the vegetable curries.

✚ F4 ✉ 56 Race Course Road ☎ 6293 8682 🕒 Daily 10.30–10 🚇 Little India

CHIN WAH HENG SEAFOOD ($$)

Popular dishes, including Chili Crab, are on the menu at this long-established East Coast restaurant. Kids are especially welcome here.

✚ M5 ✉ 01–01 East Coast Seafood Centre, Block 1202 East Coast Parkway ☎ 6444 7967 🕒 Daily 5pm–midnight 🚇 Eunos, then bus 55 or 105 🚌 16, 55, 76, 135, 155

COLOURS BY THE BAY ($$)

A novel dining experience, since it brings together many cuisines under one roof, from Chinese to Korean, Thai, Italian and fusion.

✚ F6 ✉ 1–13A/G Esplanade Mall, 8 Raffles Avenue ☎ 6341 9985 🕒 Daily 11.30–2.30, 6–11 🚇 Millenia

EAST COAST LAGOON FOOD CENTRE ($)

The good food and sea breezes make this popular. The satay is very good, as are the *laksa* and any number of tantalizing seafood dishes, including chili or black pepper crab.

✚ d3 ✉ East Coast Parkway 🕒 Late morning until late daily 🚇 Bugis, then bus 401 (Sat, Sun, holidays only)

IMPERIAL HERBAL RESTAURANT ($$$)

Ants and scorpions, anyone? You'll find them on the menu here.

✚ F5 ✉ Metropole Hotel, 41 Seah Street ☎ 6337 0491 🕒 Daily 11.30–2.30, 6.30–10.30 🚇 City Hall

JUMBO SEAFOOD ($$$)

Lots of tasty seafood dishes, but renown for its chili crab.

✚ d3 ✉ 1208 East Coast Parkway ☎ 6442 3435 🕒 Daily 11.30–2, 6–11 🚇 Eunos, then bus 55 or 105 🚌 16, 55, 76, 135, 155

STEAMBOAT

Not a form of transportation, rather a delicious method of tableside cooking where a selection of fish, meat and vegetables is placed in a container of boiling broth; you can cook it to your liking and retrieve it with chopsticks when it's achieved perfect readiness.

LEI GARDEN ($$$)

The CHIJMES branch of this upscale chain serves Cantonese specialties such as Beijing duck.

✚ F5 ✉ 01–24 Chijmes, 30 Victoria Street ☎ 6339 3822 🕒 Daily 11.30– 2.30, 6–10.30 🚇 City Hall

MANGO TREE ($$)

Popular beachside location and delicious southern Indian cuisine, plus sunset views.

✚ d3 ✉ 1000 East Coast Parkway ☎ 6442 8655 🕒 Daily 11.30–2.30, 6.30–11 🚇 Eunos, then bus 55 or 105 🚌 16, 55, 76, 135, 155

SKETCHES PASTA & WINE BAR ($)

Set around the kitchen, the idea of this friendly place is that you design your own pasta dishes from a list of fresh ingredients.

✚ F5 ✉ 200 Victoria Street, 01–85 Parco Bugis Junction ☎ 6339 8386 🕒 Daily 11–10 🚇 Bugis

WAK LOK CANTONESE RESTAURANT ($$)

Fine Cantonese dinners and tasty dim sum lunches. Hong Kong Chinese come here to eat.

✚ F5 ✉ Carlton Hotel, 76 Bras Basah Road ☎ 6311 8188 🕒 Mon–Sat 11.30–2.30, 6.30–10.30, Sun 11–2.30, 6.30–10.30 🚇 City Hall

RESTAURANTS

EAST ISLAND

Singapore is so close to exciting Malaysian and Indonesian destinations that, if you have time, you should experience the exotic differences offered by some of the cities, ports and resorts of the area.

Sights	**96–99**	Top 25	**TOP 25**
Diving Singapore's Islands	**100–101**	Pulau Ubin ▷ **96**	
Excursions	**102–103**		
Walk	**104**		
Shopping	**106**		
Restaurants	**106**		

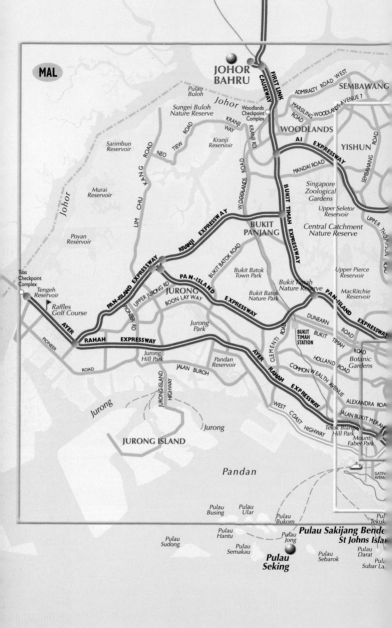

MAL

JOHOR BAHRU

Pulau Buloh

Johor

Sungei Buloh Nature Reserve

Woodlands Checkpoint Complex

FIRST LINK

CAUSEWAY

ADMIRALTY ROAD WEST

SEMBAWANG

MARSILING

WOODLANDS AVENUE 7

WOODLANDS ROAD

KRANJI WAY

KRANJI RD

Kranji Reservoir

NEO TIEW ROAD

LIM CHU KANG ROAD

WOODLANDS

A1 EXPRESSWAY

MANDAI ROAD

YISHUN

SEMBAWANG ROAD

Sarimbun Reservoir

Singapore Zoological Gardens

Upper Seletor Reservoir

Central Catchment Nature Reserve

UPPER THOMSON ROAD

Johor

Murai Reservoir

WOODLANDS ROAD

BUKIT TIMAH EXPRESSWAY

BUKIT PANJANG

Poyan Reservoir

KRANJI EXPRESSWAY

Bukit Batok Road

Bukit Batok Town Park

Upper Pierce Reservoir

Tuas Checkpoint Complex

PAN-ISLAND EXPRESSWAY

PAN-ISLAND

UPPER JURONG RD

JURONG

BOON LAY WAY

Bukit Batok Nature Park

Bukit Timah Nature Reserve

MacRitchie Reservoir

PAN-ISLAND EXPRESSWAY

ROAD

Tengeh Reservoir

Raffles Golf Course

EXPRESSWAY

PIONEER RD

Jurong Park

DUNEARN ROAD

BUKIT TIMAH STATION

BUKIT TIMAH ROAD

AYER RAHAH EXPRESSWAY

PIONEER ROAD

Jurong Hill Park

JALAN BUROH

Pandan Reservoir

CLEMENTI ROAD

HOLLAND ROAD

Botanic Gardens

JURONG ISLAND HIGHWAY

AYER RAHAH EXPRESSWAY

COMMONWEALTH AVENUE

ALEXANDRA ROAD

Jurong

Jurong

WEST COAST HIGHWAY

JALAN BUKIT MERAH

Telok Blangah Hill Park

Mount Faber Park

JURONG ISLAND

GATEV AVENI

Pandan

Pulau Busing

Pulau Ular

Pulau Bukom

Pul Tekuk

Pulau Sakijang Bende St Johns Islan

Pulau Hantu

Pulau Jong

Pulau Sudong

Pulau Semakau

Pulau Sebarok

Pulau Darat

Pulau Seking

Pula Subar La

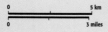

0   5 km

0   3 miles

MAL

Sembawang
Beach

*Pulau
Seletar*

Johor

*Pulau
Punggol Barat*

*Pulau
Punggol Timor*

ishun
Park

*Pulau
Serangoon*

Mamam Beach

Orchid
Country Club

Seletar
Airport

PUNGGOL

Pulau Ubin
Beach

Desaru

ower Seletar
Reservoir

Coney Island
Beach

Pulau Ubin

*Pulau Ubin
Park*

TAMPINES   EXPRESSWAY

*Pulau
Ketam*

Changi
Beach

ANG
MO KIO

CENTRAL   EXPRESSWAY

ANG MO   KIO   AVENUE 5

SENGKANG
HOUGANG

PUNGGOL ROAD

PASIR
RIS

Pasir Ris
Beach

*Serangoon
Harbour*

TAMPINES

ROAD

*Pasir Ris
Park*

CHANGI

Changi
International
Airport

ROAD

HOUGANG ROAD

SERANGOON AVENUE

TAMPINES

TAMPINES AVENUE 10

EXPRESSWAY   LOYANG AVENUE

BISHAN

UPPER   SERANGOON

BARTLEY RD

*Bedok
Reservoir*

PAN-ISLAND   EXPRESSWAY

SIMEI

AIRPORT   BOULEVARD

CHANGI COAST ROAD

TOA
PAYOH

ROAD

NEW   UPPER   CHANGI   ROAD

CHANGI
EAST

SINGAPORE

BEDOK

ROAD

COAST   PARKWAY

*Safra
Golf Course*

EAST   COAST   COAST

EAST

East Coast Beach

Marine Cove

NJONG PAGAR
ATION

*East Coast
Park*

*Pulau
Brani*

entosa

*Pulau
Seringat*

**Pulau Tembakul
Kusu**

*Pulau Sakijang Pelepah
Lazarus*

Pulau Ubin

HIGHLIGHTS

- Groves of coconuts
- Old rubber plantation
- Mangrove swamps
- Hiking

TIP

- Be sure to take insect repellent and sunscreen, as well as a good hat.

This undeveloped island just northeast of the mainland is a rural idyll compared to the concrete and consumerism of Singapore. You can wander through coconut groves and even mangrove swamps.

Eating and drinking Just off the jetty at Pulau Ubin there is an endearingly scruffy little village where you can enjoy Malay and Chinese specialties. The Ubin Information Kiosk, run by National Parks, is located near the jetty and has free maps and information on interesting places to visit. You have a choice of walking or renting a bicycle for a leisurely trip around the island. There are drink stalls all over the island, offering cold drinks as well as coconut milk straight from the coconut. Pulau Ubin's many fruit orchards produce delicious durian, mangosteens and rambutans in season.

Clockwise from top left: fishing on Pulau Ubin; a local bungalow on the island; cycle tours are available on the island; Kelongs (wooden houses above the water on stilts) can still be seen on Pulau Ubin

Wildlife and temples Keep an eye out for local bird life in the mangrove swamps and forests. Pulau Ubin is very poplular with bird-watchers. Several hornbills make their home on the island, as well as the Red Junglefowl, the wild ancestor of the domestic chicken. You can visit traditional temples and shrines as you make your way around the island. You'll find the Lotus Pond Temple just after the bridge over Sungei Jelutong. The pond near the temple is a beautiful sight when the flowers are in bloom.

Chek Jawa Any walk will take you by the sites of old limestone quarries, but Chek Jawa is the most visited coastal area on the island. Here you can explore the natural rocky shoreline, mangroves and beaches—look for the sand bar where you'll find starfish, crabs and sand dollars at low tide.

THE BASICS

✚ e2

🚇 MRT to Tampines then bus 29 to Changi Village interchange. It's a 10-min bumboat ride from Changi Jetty (near the Changi Village Hawker Centre) to the jetty at Pulau Ubin. Bumboats operate from 6am to 11pm

✋ Bumboat ticket inexpensive

❓ Nature walks, bird-watching and cycling tours run by the Green Volunteers Network www.gvn.com.sg. Free guided walks organized by National Parks ☎ 6542 4108, 6545 4761

More to See

DESARU

www.myoutdoor.com

Located on the eastern tip of the Malaysian peninsula, Desaru is a popular beach resort for Singaporeans, and a good introduction to Malaysian culture. Its casuarina-lined, clean, sandy white beaches are fringed by lush tropical forest. There are numerous resorts and hotels—activities include golfing, horse riding, tennis, canoeing, swimming, boating, fishing and snorkeling.

✚ Off map ✉ 78 miles (125km) northeast of Singapore. Accessible from Singapore by road via Kota Tinggi (2-hour drive), and by ferry from Changi Ferry Terminal, Mon–Thu, 3 times a day and Fri–Sun, 4 times a day ☎ 6546 8518

PULAU SEKING

As you travel to the island, you pass lots of freight ships awaiting berth in Singapore's busy harbor. The island has a small Malay settlement of brightly painted, stilt houses that stand over the sea. You may walk around the settlement and, since some villagers sell drinks, shells and coral, it's worth buying something just to get a look inside the traditional houses.

✚ b–c4 ✉ 5 miles (8km) southwest of Singapore ⛴ 60-min ferry ride from Marina South Pier. Departure times: 10 and 1.30 (Mon–Sat) and 9, 11, 1, 3 and 5 (Sun and public holidays) ☎ 1800-736 8672 (freephone in Singapore)

ST. JOHN'S ISLAND

Just 0.6 miles (km) south of the southernmost part of Sentosa, St. John's Island (formerly known as Pulau Sekijang Bendara) is a former penal settlement with idyllic, clean, sandy beaches, walking tracks and lagoons for swimming. The low-key holiday bungalows, which can accommodate 10 people, have low rents and the picnic grounds are perfect for day-trippers.

✚ c4 ✉ 4 miles (6.5km) south of Singapore ⛴ 45-min ferry ride from Marina South Pier. Departure times: 10 and 1.30 (Mon–Sat) and 9, 11, 1, 3 and 5 (Sun and public holidays) ☎ 1800-736 8672 (freephone in Singapore)

St. John's Island

Diving Singapore's Islands

Orpheus Dive Centre is a PADI 5-Star Dive Center offering scuba diving courses, ranging from beginner to professional levels. They offer "learning how to scuba dive" courses from S$350. Weekly classes are held in popular West Malaysian destinations such as Pulau Tioman and Pulau Dayang. www.orpheusdive.com

☎ 6292 0096

✉ 184A, Telok Ayer Street, Singapore

Some of Singapore's offshore islands are suitable for scuba diving, although due to often strong currents, divers should take organized tours. Local dive schools conduct NAUI or PADI courses with day and night diving options.

Kusu Island

The island's two swimming lagoons are a popular destination for day-trippers. The warm fringing waters are ideal for swimming among hard and soft corals, pelagic fish, sea fans, sea snakes and turtles. Dolphins are sometimes seen.

Visit the charming Chinese Temple, Da Ba Gong (Temple of the Merchant God), which attracts 130,000 people on the ninth month of lunar calendar, and the Malay shrine Kramat Kusu. And be sure to take in the stunning views of the mainland from the hilltop.

✚ Southeast of Sentosa

🚢 Ferry from Marina South Pier. Departure times: 10 and 1.30 (Mon to Sat), and at 9, 11, 1, 3 and 5 (Sun and public holidays)

💵 Return ticket S$9 adults, S$6 children 3 to 12 years

☎ 1800-736 8672 (freephone in Singapore)

Average Visibility: 3ft (1m)

Maximum Depth: 100ft (30m)

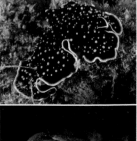

A six-banded angelfish (above) and a marine flatworm (above right)

A squid

Lazarus Island and Sisters' Island

These two tiny islands, just south of Singapore, have sandy beaches and are perfect for swimming, snorkeling and scuba diving. Since the currents are strong, divers should be experienced. On the southern tip of Lazarus Island there is a wreck at 60ft (18m). Sisters' Island has a shallow reef at 20ft (6m) and a wreck at 70ft (21m).

Lazarus Island

➕ Between St. John's Island and Kusu Island
🚢 Ferry from Marina South Pier. Departure times: 10 and 1.30 (Mon–Sat), and 9, 11, 1, 3 and 5 (Sun and public holidays)
💵 Return ticket S$9 adults, S$6 children 3 to 12 years
☎ 1800-736 8672 (freephone in Singapore)
Average Visibility: 3ft (1m)
Maximum Depth: 60ft (18m)

Sisters' Island

➕ South of Sentosa
🚢 Ferry from Marina South Pier. Departure times: 10 and 1.30 (Mon–Sat), and 9, 11, 1, 3 and 5 (Sun and public holidays)
💵 Return ticket S$9 adults, S$6 children 3 to 12 years
☎ 1800-736 8672 (freephone in Singapore)
Average Visibility: 5ft (1.5m)
Maximum Depth: 70ft (21m)

SURVIVING

Traveling to the islands and getting around them is hot, thirsty work and you need to understand how to prevent dehydration and how to notice if you have it. On a hot day, it may take as little as 15 minutes to become dehydrated and the following are signs: dry lips and tongue, apathy and lack of energy, muscle cramping, and bright-color or dark urine.

To prevent dehydration:
● Wear loose, light-color clothing.
● Drink plenty of water
● Consume ample electrolytes
● Cool off by pouring some water over your head and neck.

A tigertail seahorse

An icon seastar

Excursions

THE BASICS

➕ Off map to southeast
🚢 Ferries leave Singapore Cruise Centre (6270 2228) and Tanah Merah Ferry Terminal (6276 9722) several times a day—the trip takes about 45 min
Channel Holidays Pte Ltd
☎ 6270 2228
Auto Batam Ferries & Tours Pte Ltd ☎ 6271 4866
Bintan Resort Ferries
☎ 6542 4369
💵 Expensive

BINTAN

Bintan Island is about 28 miles (45km) southeast of Singapore, in the Riau Archipelago, the third largest province of Indonesia. An excellent excursion from Singapore, the island provides an introduction to Indonesian culture and, although the friendly locals speak Bahasa Indonesian, they enjoy practicing their English.

North and South Numerous seaside resorts, hotels and chalets, catering to a wide range of budgets, cover the northern shores of the island and are separated from the rest of the island by checkpoints and security guards. The southern part of the island is more populated and industrial, with electronics factories, fishing villages and bustling towns with thousands of motorcycles.

Island life Tanjung Pinang is the largest town on the island. The old, central market area, built on stilts, is a fascinating place and small enough to walk around. Try the delicious local fruit and seafood, and browse the interesting shops and markets. Pulau Penyengat, a 10-minute bumboat ride from Tanjung Pinang pier, has a charming fishing village, the remains of an old palace, and a mosque dating from 1880.

Practicalities Time is one hour behind Singapore time. Bring cash in rupiah for use in the local shops and street stalls; Singapore dollars and credit cards are also accepted for accommodation and food. Make sure you have your passport and check to see if you need a visa for entry. Most travelers can get a visa on arrival (VOA). Once you arrive, you fill in an arrival/departure card and pay US$10 for a 7-day stay—more for longer.

JOHOR BAHRU

Johor Bahru is at the southern tip of the Malay Peninsula, just a short ride across the causeway from Singapore. Also referred to as JB, the state capital of Johor is a thriving commercial and administrative centre, with many shopping malls, hotels, restaurants and entertainment venues.

Choices Hotels in the city suit every taste and budget—there are resorts, international hotels and budget accommodations. Numerous nightclubs, discos, karaokes and three cinemas can be found in the heart of the city and, after sunset, a sumptuous array of food stalls appear along the streets. There are also plenty of hawker centers and restaurants offering traditional Malay, Indian and Chinese delicacies.

Shopping and sightseeing The favorable exchange rate and tempting bargains in the big shopping malls, handicraft centers, bazaars and markets make JB a popular shopping destination with Singaporeans and overseas tourists. The Royal Sultan Abu Bakar Museum (Grand Palace) and its immaculate gardens, the beautiful Sultan Abu Bakar Mosque, and the Johor Art Gallery are some of JB's more famous historical and cultural attractions. The city is also a good point of departure for Malaysia's East Coast.

How to get there Take a Malaysian taxi from Rochor Road, where you can share a taxi, or book a specially licensed Singapore taxi. Buses run regularly from the Queen Street terminal in central Singapore. A ferry link operates daily between Changi Point near the Singapore International Airport and Tanjung Belungkor in Johor.

THE BASICS

➕ b1
Malaysia Tourism Promotion Board:
www.tourism.gov.my
✉ 2 Jalan Ayer Molek, Johor Bahru 80000, Johor
☎ 607 222 3590 / 3591
Fax: 607 223 5502
Taxi: Johor Taxi Service
☎ 6296 7054

Royal Sultan Abu Bakar Museum
✉ Jalan Tun Dr. Ismail, 15-min walk west of border
☎ 607 223 0555
🕐 Sat–Thu 9–4
💷 Inexpensive

FARTHER AFIELD

EXCURSIONS

Pulau Ubin
Sensory Trail

Pack sunblock and water, and head to the Sensory Trail, which displays Asian plants used for food, medicines and everyday items.

DISTANCE: 1 mile (1.5km) **ALLOW:** 60–90 min, best attempted early in the day

START **END**

PULAU UBIN JETTY
✚ e2 🚇 Tampines, then bus 29 to Changi Village. 10-min bumboat ride from Changi Jetty to the jetty at Pulau Ubin

PULAU UBIN JETTY

❶ Walk through the little village that surrounds the jetty to the Visitors Centre, just a short distance from the jetty, on the right. Ask at the Centre for a map of the walk.

❻ Take the trail back to the center of the main village for a look around the shops, a fresh tropical fruit drink and a delicious seafood meal. Have a rest in the shade before you head back to the mainland.

❷ The trail starts in the Spice and Herb Garden at the back of the Visitors Centre, with a walk alongside a cool, shady banana grove. This useful plant is a good source of energy and vitamins and the leaves are used as food wrappers and disposable plates.

❺ Next you'll visit the island's coconut plantations, where you can take a break and buy a cold drink or try some fresh coconut milk, straight from the coconut.

❸ The pathway continues past a huge field of fragrant pandan. The scented leaves are often used in Asian cooking for coloring and flavoring. Next are plantings of the grass citronella, long leafstalks of torch ginger, curry trees, climbing beans, passionfruit, guava, Aloe vera, the elephant yam, and finally a grove of sugarcane.

❹ The trail goes on to the second section of the walk, which takes you through coastal forest and mangrove habitat. Here you'll see spiky pandanus (the leaves are used to make mats and baskets), mangrove trees, sea hibiscus (strings and cords are made from the bark), and betel nut palms (the nut is used in traditional Malay medicine).

Shopping

BINTAN MALL
You'll find a variety of clothing, specialty and gift stores, and lots of stalls selling tasty Indonesian food at this bustling mall.

➕ Off map to south
✉ Jalan Pos, Tanjung Pinang, Bintan ☎ 62 7731 8041
🕐 Daily 10–10

JOHOR BAHRU DUTY FREE COMPLEX (ZON)
www.zon.com.my
The largest duty-free complex in Malaysia is packed with electronic goods, clothing and brand-name goods of all descriptions. Just 1.2 miles (2km) from the Singapore Causeway, ZON is easily accessible via daily international ferry services from Tanah Merah in Singapore.

➕ Off map to west ✉ 88 Jalan Ibrahim Sultan Stulang Laut, Johor Bahru ☎ 607227 4045 🕐 Daily 11–10
🚌 Regular buses from Customs area 6am–11pm

PLAZA PELANGI
A multitude of stores offer a wide array of value-for-money quality merchandise, from handicraft items and souvenirs to large selections of fashion apparel, accessories and trendy footwear. There are also eateries, a patisserie and fast-food outlets.

➕ Off map to west ✉ 2 Jalan Kuning, Taman Pelangi, Johor Bahru ☎ 607 218 1818
🕐 Daily 10–10 🚌 Regular buses from Customs area 6am–11pm

Restaurants

PRICES
Prices are approximate, based on a 3-course meal for one person.
$$$	over S$50
$$	S$20–S$50
$	under S$20

BANYAN TREE BINTAN ($$$)
www.banyantree.com
The finest luxury beach resort this side of Bali has a wealth of restaurant options that are worth the trip Bintan. There are three restaurants—Saffron, Treetops and The Cove—but the real attractions are the exclusive dining packages, which involve candlelit meals-for-two beside the South China Sea in the most private extremities of the resort.

➕ Off map ✉ Jalan Teluk Berembang Laguna Bintan, Lagoi, Bintan, Indonesia
☎ 62 770 693 100 🕐 Daily 6.30am–10.30pm. Private dinners after 6pm every night

NEW HONG KONG RESTAURANT ($)
A popular Cantonese restaurant, housed in two double-story shophouses with Oriental decor, specializes in dim sum and a variety of fish, poultry and vegetable dishes.

➕ 1b ✉ 69–A Jalan Ibrahim Sultan, Johor Bahru
☎ 607 222 2608 🕐 Daily 12–2.30, 6–10.30

SEASON 'LIVE' SEAFOOD ($$)
Sit at makeshift tables, sip fresh coconut juice and enjoy a seafood dinner of steamed king prawns, tofu seafood soup, and crabs fried with spicy black pepper.

➕ 2e ✉ 59E Pulau Ubin, Singapore ☎ 6542 7627
🕐 Daily 12–2, 5–10

TAMAN SRI TEBRAU HAWKER CENTRE ($)
Around 50 stalls sell the best Malaysian fare to be found under one roof. Try Penang-fried *kuay teow*, satay or Hokkien prawn *mee*.

➕ Off map to west ✉ Jalan Keris, Johor Bahru ☎ 607 218 1818 🕐 Daily 10–10

In Singapore you'll find some of the world's best hotels, such as Raffles, while at lower prices, places such as YMCA International House offer comfortable and clean accommodation in a prime location.

Introduction	**108**
Budget Hotels	**109**
Mid-Range Hotels	**110–111**
Luxury Hotels	**112**

Where to Stay

Introduction

Singapore is a city that caters to the whole range of accommodation styles and price ranges. Choose from backpacker hostels and boutique hotels through to top-of-the-range five-star quality hotels such as the Mandarin Oriental or historic Raffles. All are very well equipped and offer standard room facilities as well as fitness centers and spas in the more exclusive places.

Business Options

For those who want to keep in touch with the business world while they are here, most hotels have international direct-dial telephones in rooms and Internet and cable access also. In many instances there are business facilities within the premises where remote meetings and conferences can take place. Whatever your needs and preferences, there will be a hotel here that fits your particular bill and purse.

Reservations

Be sure to make advance reservations to avoid having to compromise your budget by missing out on the low and mid-range accommodations, which are often fully booked. Of course, the Internet is the way to go for bookings, and there are often seasonal specials on offer. And if you do arrive without prior reservations, the SHA counters at the airport will help you find a place to stay.

The STB's website (www.visitsingapore.com) also has a fantastic interactive booking service.

The choice of accomodation options in Singapore is excellent

STAY AT THE AIRPORT

There are many reasons—delayed flight, lost booking, convenience—why you might like to stay at Singapore's international airport. Fortunately, all three terminals at Changi Airort have their own transit hotel, where for around S$60 per night you can rest in comfort, shower and change, swim in the pool, have a massage, or use the business center, all without the hassle of immigration and customs clearance, and without worrying about getting to the airport to catch your ongoing flight.

Budget Hotels

PRICES

Expect to pay under S$100 per person per night for a budget hotel.

BEN COOLEN

www.hotelbencoolen.com
This 74-room budget hotel is near the Singapore Art Museum and Little India and not far from Orchard Road and the Marina area.
✚ F5 ✉ 47 Bencoolen Street ☎ 6336 0822 🚇 Dhoby Ghaut

BROADWAY

A Serangoon Road location puts this hotel in the middle of the Little India district. Standards are high and the staff friendly. Good Indian restaurant next door.
✚ F4 ✉ 195 Serangoon Road ☎ 6292 4661; fax 6291 6414 🚇 Bugis

LITTLE INDIA GUEST HOUSE

Facilities are basic—all rooms share a bathroom and there's no café or bar—but the location is right in the heart of Little India. Good if your budget is limited.
✚ F4 ✉ 3 Veerasamy Road ☎ 6294 2866; fax 6298 4866 🚇 Little India

LLOYD'S INN

www.lloydinn.com
Definitely budget accommodation, but all rooms are air-conditioned and have a phone and en-suite bathrooms. There are no recreational or business facilities, but there is a launderette.
✚ D5 ✉ 2 Lloyd Road ☎ 6737 7309 🚇 Somerset

METROPOLE

www.metrohotel.com
This hotel, across the street from Raffles, is a cut above basic. The famed Imperial Herbal Restaurant (▷ 92) is here.
✚ F5 ✉ 41 Seah Street ☎ 6336 3611; fax 6339 3610 🚇 City Hall

METROPOLITAN YMCA

www.mymca.org.sg
One of a number of YMCAs in Singapore, with a swimming pool. Book ahead.

INEXPENSIVE STAYS

Singapore, unlike many Asian cities, does not have a plethora of good, inexpensive accommodations. Some of the places on this page charge around S$100 per night per room, and are of a good standard. There are cheaper establishments, especially around Bencoolen Street, and some dormitory-style hostels, known as "crash pads," but the standards of cleanliness and privacy can be quite low. The STB booklet entitled Budget Hotels lists a number of places that charge less than S$60 per night.

✚ C3 ✉ 60 Stevens Road ☎ 6839 8333 🚇 MRT to Orchard then bus 196, 190, 132, 105, 605

NEW 7TH STOREY HOTEL

Close to Bugis MRT, this hostel/hotel offers air-conditioned rooms and dormitories.
✚ F5 ✉ 229 Rocher Road ☎ 6737 0251; fax 6334 3550 🚇 Bugis

RELC INTERNATIONAL HOTEL

www.relcih.com.sg
Excellent value and location—Orchard Road is 10 minutes away. All rooms have a TV, a big bathroom, fridge and a balcony.
✚ C4 ✉ 30 Orange Grove Road ☎ 6885 7888 🚇 Orchard

STRAND

www.strandhotel.com.sg
A budget hotel with café and ensuite bathrooms.
✚ F5 ✉ 25 Bencoolen Street ☎ 6338 1866 🚇 Dhoby Ghaut

YMCA INTERNATIONAL HOUSE

www.mymca.org.sg
This YMCA, with a prime location near the start of Orchard Road, has a fitness facility and pool, and a McDonald's is in the building. Reserve well in advance.
✚ E5 ✉ 1 Orchard Road ☎ 6336 6000 🚇 Dhoby Ghaut

Mid-Range Hotels

PRICES

Expect to pay between S$100 and S$250 per person night for a mid-range hotel.

ALBERT COURT HOTEL

www.albertcourt.com.sg
An eight-floor hotel comprising 136 rooms in a renovated shophouse near Little India, with café and good facilities.
🏨 F5 ✉ 180 Albert Street ☎ 6339 3939 🚇 Bugis

ALLSON HOTEL SINGAPORE

www.allsonhotels.com
Well placed in the Historic District, this hotel features elegant carved rosewood furniture in all of the guest rooms. Also has a small pool area and gym.
🏨 F5 ✉ 101 Victoria Street ☎ 6336 0811 🚇 Bugis Junction

BERJAYA DUXTON HOTEL

www.berjayahotels-resorts.com
This classy hotel is a converted shophouse. It has one of the best French restaurants in town, which supplies excellent breakfasts (included in the room price) and dinners.
🏨 E8 ✉ 83 Duxton Road ☎ 6227 7678 🚇 Tanjong Pagar

CONCORDE HOTEL SINGAPORE

www.concorde.net
A bit out of the way in Chinatown, but very reasonably priced. Outdoor pool and tennis court, two restaurants and a bar, a business area, 24-hour room service and babysitting.
🏨 D7 ✉ 317 Outram Road ☎ 6733 0188 🚇 Chinatown

THE ELIZABETH SINGAPORE

www.theelizabeth.com
This small, comfortable hotel features a three-story-high series of waterfalls. Excellent value and good location. Restaurant, small outdoor pool and fitness area, 24-hour room service and babysitting.
🏨 D4 ✉ 24 Mount Elizabeth ☎ 6738 1188 🚇 Orchard

EXCELSIOR HOTEL

Very well located, with Chinatown, the colonial Civic District, Boat Quay,

LOCATION

Singapore's mid-range hotels are scattered throughout the city center, and it is worth trying to find a hotel that suits your sightseeing tastes as much as your budget. Shoppers could consider the many Orchard Road and surrounds options, while lovers of Chinese art and culture may find that staying in Chinatown provides plenty of opportunity to seek out architectural and cultural aspects of Singapore that are fast disappearing.

Clarke Quay and Marina Bay all a stone's throw away. Swimming pool.
🏨 F6 ✉ 3–5 Coleman Street ☎ 6337 2200; fax 6339 3847 🚇 City Hall

FURAMA HOTEL SINGAPORE

www.furama-hotels.com
In a great location in Chinatown, near Boat Quay and Clarke Quay, where there's plenty of shopping, dining and nightlife. Outdoor pool, two restaurants, non-smoking rooms, and fitness and business facilities.
🏨 E7 ✉ 60 Eu Tong Sen Street ☎ 6533 3888 🚇 Chinatown

GARDEN HOTEL

This pleasant hotel is slightly off the beaten track, but represents very good value, with the facilities of a much fancier place, including a pool. Within walking distance of Orchard and Scotts roads.
🏨 C4 ✉ 14 Balmoral Road, Bukit Timah ☎ 6235 3344; fax 6235 9730 🚇 Newton

HOTEL GRAND CENTRAL

www.grandcentral.com.sg
Right in the Orchard Road area, this hotel is very popular, so make sure you book in advance. Has a restaurant, outdoor pool, fitness area, tour desk and business facilities.
🏨 E5 ✉ 22 Cavenagh Road ☎ 6737 9944 🚇 Dhoby Ghaut

HOTEL WINDSOR
www.hotelwindsor.com.sg
Good value for the money and easy access to the East Coast make this a popular choice. The Cafe Windsor serves continental cuisine and tasty local fare.
➕ K1 ✉ 401 Macpherson Road ☎ 6343 0088 🚇 Aljunied

INN AT TEMPLE STREET
www.theinn.com.sg
Right in the heart of Chinatown, this charming hotel has traditional Peranakan furniture in the lobby and guest rooms. Its café serves Western and Asian dishes.
➕ E7 ✉ 36 Temple Street, Chinatown ☎ 6221 5333 🚌 84, 166, 197

PENINSULA EXCELSIOR
www.ytchotels.com.sg
Top value for money. An excellent location in the Historic District and you can walk to Chinatown from here. Restaurant and bar, two outdoor pools, babysitting, fitness and business facilities.
➕ F6 ✉ 5 Coleman Street ☎ 6337 2200 🚇 City Hall

PLAZA HOTEL
www.plazapacifichotels.com
Excellent leisure facilities here—a half-size Olympic pool and Balinese-style spa, café and sun-deck. Also two gyms, a sauna and a steam room.
➕ F5 ✉ 7500A Beach Road ☎ 6298 0011 🚇 Bugis

ROYAL
www.hotelroyal.com.sg
One of Singapore's older hotels, with spacious rooms at very good rates. A five-minute walk from Novena MRT and, in the other direction, the famous Newton Circus hawker center. Swimming pool.
➕ D3 ✉ 36 Newton Road ☎ 6426 0168; fax 6235 8668 🚇 Novena

ROYAL PEACOCK HOTEL
www.royalpeaockhotel.com
Nestled in a row of converted shophouses in Chinatown's relatively low-key, red-light district, the Royal Peacock is awash with European furniture and deep carpets, and bed linens are plum

---

TRAVEL TO YOUR HOTEL

Besides Singapore's modern and efficient public transportation system, taxis are everywhere and very affordable. Another convenient way to travel to and from Singapore's Changi Airport is to take a six-seater MaxiCab shuttle service, which operates daily from 6am to midnight. The service stops at Concorde Hotel Singapore, Crown Prince Hotel Singapore, Excelsior Peninsula Hotel and Marina Mandarin Singapore and has a flexible routing system between the airport and hotels within the city.

---

and emerald green.
➕ E7 ✉ 55 Keong Saik Road ☎ 6223 3522 🚇 Outram Park

SWISSÔTEL MERCHANT COURT HOTEL
www.singapore-merchant-court.com
This hotel, on the Singapore River between Clarke Quay and Chinatown, is always a good choice. The extensive facilities include a great pool, a business center, self-service laundry facilities and a relaxing lobby bar.
➕ E6 ✉ 20 Merchant Road ☎ 6337 2288 🚇 Clarke Quay

TRADERS HOTEL
This is near the Botanic Gardens and Orchard Road. Family apartments have small kitchens and rooms with foldaway beds that double as meeting rooms for business travelers.
➕ C4 ✉ 1A Cuscaden Road ☎ 6738 2222; fax 6831 4314 🚇 Orchard

YORK HOTEL SINGAPORE
www.yorkhotel.com.sg
A small hotel with spacious rooms, just a short walk from Orchard Road. Restaurant, outdoor pool and sun deck with huge palms, 24-room service and babysitting.
➕ D4 ✉ 21 Mount Elizabeth ☎ 6737 0511 🚇 Orchard

Luxury Hotels

FOUR SEASONS

www.fourseasons.com/singapore

Ideally located just behind Orchard Road, with top-notch facilities, two pools, air-conditioned tennis courts and good restaurants.

➕ C4 ✉ 190 Orchard Boulevard ☎ 6734 1110 🚇 Orchard

FULLERTON

www.fullertonhotel.com

Located in the heritage GPO building, the Fullerton has lovely river views.

➕ F7 ✉ 1 Fullerton Square ☎ 6735 8388 🚇 Raffles Place

GOODWOOD PARK

www.goodwoodparkhotel.com.sg

Formerly the Teutonia Club for German expatriates, this hotel retains its charm. It is well located, close to Orchard Road, and has lovely gardens.

➕ C4 ✉ 22 Scotts Road ☎ 6737 7411 🚇 Orchard

MARINA MANDARIN

With a superb waterfront location in the Marina Bay, this 575-room luxury hotel offers the ultimate in facilities, including a host of recreation possibilities.

➕ F6 ✉ 6 Raffles Boulevard ☎ 6845 1000; fax 6845 1199 🚇 City Hall

MARRIOTT

www.marriott.com

This Singapore landmark, formerly the Dynasty, retains its original distinctive pagoda-style roof and features a roof-top pool and business and fitness facilities. Central location above Tangs store.

➕ C4 ✉ 320 Orchard Road ☎ 6735 8967 🚇 Orchard

ORIENTAL

www.mandarin-oriental.com/singapore

The 21-floor Oriental is one of three luxury hotels built on reclaimed land overlooking Marina Bay. It is close to Marina Square shopping mall—good for last-minute gifts—and Suntec City, which incorporates one of the largest conference and exhibition halls in Asia and is Singapore's newest central business district.

➕ F6 ✉ 5 Raffles Avenue, Marina Square ☎ 6339 8811 🚇 City Hall

GOING UP!

Don't miss the ride in the high-speed elevator of the Swissôtel the Stamford—the only way to get to the top of its 73 floors. A matter of seconds after leaving the ground you are deposited 741ft (226m) above street level.

RAFFLES

www.raffles.com

To relive the golden age of travel, stay at Raffles (▷ 38), Singapore's most famous hotel, first opened in 1887. All the accommodations are suites and are expensive.

➕ F5 ✉ 1 Beach Road ☎ 6337 1886 🚇 City Hall

RITZ-CARLTON MILLENIA

www.ritzcarlton.com

Ideal for business travelers and for visitors who can afford to splurge. A commanding position on Marina Bay provides fantastic views over the harbor and the new Esplanade theater complex.

➕ F6 ✉ 7 Raffles Avenue ☎ 6337 8888 🚇 City Hall

SHANGRI-LA

www.shangri-la.com

One of Singapore's finest hotels, with all the facilities you'd expect, plus magnificent gardens and a golf putting green.

➕ B3 ✉ 22 Orange Grove Road ☎ 6737 3644 🚇 Orchard

SWISSÔTEL THE STAMFORD

www.swissotel.com

Reputedly the tallest hotel in the world outside the United States, this luxury hotel has every possible amenity, including 16 restaurants, a business center, sports facilities and views.

➕ F6 ✉ 2 Stamford Road ☎ 6338 8585 🚇 City Hall

Need to Know

The more you plan your trip, the more you'll get out of your time in Singapore. Try to catch Chinese New Year (January/February), Singapore Food Festival (March), or the Great Singapore Sale (July).

Planning Ahead	114–115
Getting There	116–117
Getting Around	118–119
Essential Facts	120–121
Language	122
Timeline	124–125

Planning Ahead

When to Go

The best time to visit Singapore is around Chinese New Year, although you will need to book a hotel well in advance. July is sale time in Orchard Road, so shoppers take note. Otherwise, the city hums along year-round, catering to holiday and business travelers alike.

AVERAGE DAILY MAXIMUM TEMPERATURES

JAN	FEB	MAR	APR	MAY	JUN	JUL	AUG	SEP	OCT	NOV	DEC
86°F	88°F	88°F	89°F	90°F	90°F	87°F	88°F	88°F	88°F	88°F	86°F
30°C	31°C	31°C	32°C	32°C	32°C	31°C	31°C	31°C	31°C	31°C	30°C

Weather Singapore's climate is tropical, with very few seasonal variations. The temperature range is steady, from a nighttime low of 75°F (24°C) to a daily high of 88°F (31°C). December and January can be slightly cooler and May to August slightly hotter. Rainfall peaks between November and January, with the northeast monsoon. However, it rarely rains for long–usually an hour's torrential downpour at a time. During monsoon times, storms can be dramatic, with sheets of rain and intense thunder and lightning. Most occur early in the morning and in the afternoon. Humidity can sometimes reach nearly 100 percent, and averages 84 percent.

WHAT'S ON

January *River Raft Race*: All manner of rafts race on the Singapore River, plus bands, cheerleaders and food stalls.
Thaipusam: This Hindu festival displays dramatic feats of mind over matter.

January/February *Chinese New Year*: A two-day public holiday, with fireworks, stalls and dragon dances.
February Chingay Procession: A huge street carnival based on a Chinese folk festival. Lion dancers, acrobats, bands and floats.

March *Singapore Food Festival*.

April *Singapore International Film Festival*

June *Dragon Boat Festival*: 20 teams enter this longboat race.
Singapore Arts Festival: One of Asia's leading contemporary arts festivals.

July *Great Singapore Sale*: Orchard Road hosts this price-cutting month around July, to highlight Singapore as a major shopping destination.

August *National Day*: 9 August. This public holiday marks Singapore's independence from the British.

August/September *Festival of the Hungry Ghosts*: Fun and feasting.

September *Mooncake Festival*: A colorful spectacle named after the delicious mooncakes on sale.

October *Thimithi*: Fire-walking ceremony.

October/November *Festival of the Nine Emperor Gods*: A week of processions and street opera.

November *Deepavali*: Lamps are lit to celebrate the triumph of good over evil.

December *Christmas*: Orchard Road lights up.

Singapore Online

Not surprisingly, Singapore has been fully wired for broadband and has embraced the global digital culture.

www.visitsingapore.com

This dynamic site, written in 12 languages, has up-to-date details of events, exhibitions, holiday ideas and accommodations suggestions. For serious shoppers there is a list of errant retailers.

www.asia1.com.sg

Singapore's main media group's portal. Links to all major national print media websites, plus international and regional news.

www.singapore.tourism-asia.net

Plenty of up-to-date information on this site, with good sections on general travel, attractions, shopping and entertainment.

www.asiatravelmart.com

Asia's major online travel marketplace with various hotel and flight booking information, plus booking online.

www.nhb.gov.sg/MCC

Visitor information for the Asian Civilisations Museum, the Singapore Art Museum and a WWII museum at Bukit Chandu—comprehensive descriptions, photos and locations.

www.viator.com/singapore/

An excellent site where you can enter the dates of your visit and find out what's happening. Plenty of information on tours, attractions, prices and how to get there.

www.travelwithyourkids.com/destinations/?c=Singapore

This website gives a light-hearted insight into unusual things to do in Singapore that will be fun for both kids and adults.

GOOD TRAVEL SITES

www.fodors.com
A complete travel-planning site. You can research prices and weather; book air tickets, cars and rooms; ask questions (and get answers) from fellow travelers; and find links to other sites.

www.changi.airport.com.sg
Features arrival and departure details, airport facilities, and shopping and dining information in both terminals.

CYBERCAFÉS

Chills Café
F6 ✉ 01–07, 39 Stamford Road ☎ 6883 1016
🕐 Daily 9.30am–midnight
💷 S$5 per hour

Surf@Café
D5 ✉ 218 Orchard Road
☎ 6732 4154 🕐 Daily
10–10 💷 S$5 per hour

Cybernet Cafe
e2 ✉ Level 3, Terminal 2, Changi Airport ☎ 6546 1968 🕐 7am–11pm 💷 S$8 per hour

NEED TO KNOW PLANNING AHEAD

Getting There

For airport inquiries
☎ 6542 1122;
www.changiairport.com.sg.

CAR RENTAL

● Car rental is expensive and public transportation is very good.

● If you do decide to rent a car, remember that it is very expensive to take it into Malaysia; it's much better to rent one there. An area day license has to be bought to take a car into Singapore's central business district during the week and until mid-afternoon on Saturday.

● Display coupons in your windscreen in parking lots and designated parking places. Area day licenses and books of coupons can be purchased at newsagents and garages. Steep fines are incurred for failing to display licenses and coupons.

● Driving is on the left. A valid international or other recognized driving license is required.

● Insurance is included in rental fees.

AIRPORTS

Singapore's Changi Airport is 12 miles (20km) east of the city center. Flights take around 13 hours from Western Europe and around 20 hours from the US. The huge airport has two terminals, many lounges and hundreds of shops.

FROM CHANGI AIRPORT

Take the MRT train connection for easy access to all parts of the island. You can go to Tanah Merah station and switch to the westbound train service to be in the city in less than 30 minutes; the fare is S$1.40. Inquiries ☎ 1800 336 8900.

Taxi ranks are well marked and there is rarely a line. The fare into the city is around S$25.

The airport shuttle service (☎ 6553 3880) stops at major hotels in the city (journey time 30 minutes; cost S$7). It runs from 6am to midnight and can be picked up from just outside the terminal.

Public buses 16 and 36 travel to the city (6am to midnight, journey time 50 minutes; cost S$2). Pick them up below terminals 1 and 2.

ARRIVING BY BUS

Air-conditioned long-distance buses come direct from Bangkok, Penang and Kuala Lumpur, and from other main towns in the Malaysian peninsula. Singapore–Kuala Lumpur Express (☎ 6887 4347; www.asia-travel.com/coachtrain.com; journey time 6 hours; cost S$40). Fares to Bangkok are S$85

for the 28-hour journey (☎ 6294 5415), with buses leaving from the Golden Mile Complex in Beach Road.

Long-distance buses from Malaysia arrive and depart from the Lavender Street bus station. Bus 170 leaves the bus station at Johor Bahru (the Malaysian city visible across the causeway from Singapore) regularly for Ban San bus station in Singapore (Singapore–Johor Bahru Express ☎ 6292 8149; journey time 1 hour; cost S$1.90). The Second Crossing, another causeway, links Tuas in Singapore's west with Malaysia's Johor state. All bus travelers break their journeys for immigration formalities.

ARRIVING BY SEA

Most cruise ships dock at the World Trade Centre. From there, taxis and buses go to central Singapore. Ferries travel regularly between Tanjong Belungkor (Johor) and Changi ferry terminal (Ferrylink ☎ 6545 3600; journey time 45 minutes; cost S$25); to and from Tioman March to October (Auto Batam Ferries ☎ 6271 4866; journey time 4 hours 30 minutes; cost S$120); and between Harbourfront and Bintan (Auto Batam Ferries ☎ 6271 4866; journey time 1 hour 30 minutes; cost S$50).

ARRIVING BY TRAIN

There is one main north–south train line in Malaysia. Around three trains arrive per day in Singapore from Kuala Lumpur. Journey times vary but average 6 hours (for KTM timetables check www.ktmb.com.my). Immigration formalities occur once you have disembarked at Singapore's Keppel Road railway station, still technically in Malaysia (☎ 6222 5165). The Eastern and Oriental Express offers a leisurely and luxurious trip to Singapore from Bangkok, Penang or Kuala Lumpur (☎ 6392 3500).

VACCINATIONS

Vaccinations are unnecessary unless you are coming from an area infected with yellow fever or cholera.

ENTRY REQUIREMENTS

Visas are not required by citizens of the EU, US or most Commonwealth countries (although Indian visitors staying more than 4 days require a visa). Passports must be valid for at least 6 months. On arrival, tourist visas are issued for 30 days. Extensions are available from the Immigration and Checkpoints Authority ☎ 6391 6100 (10 Kallang Road) www.app.ica.gov.sg or by making a trip outside Singapore. Passport and visa regulations can change at short notice, so always check before you travel.

AIRPORT HOTEL

Terminals 1 and 2 have 73 transit hotel rooms each. Rentals are from S$56 per 6-hour block for single or double occupancy.

Getting Around

TOURIST BOARD

● Singapore Tourism produces lots of printed material about the island's attractions and tours and there are any number of brochures available from hotel reception desks. But the Touristline is handy for after-hours information and visitor centers are always worth a visit.

Touristline: ☎ 1800 736 2000 (toll-free in Singapore). (65) 6736 2000 (overseas). Little India: ✉ 73 Dunlop Street, The InnCrowd Backpackers' Hostel, ⊕ 10–10 daily ⊜ Little India

Orchard: ✉ Junction of Cairnhill Road and Orchard Road ⊕ 9.30am to 10.30pm daily ⊜ Orchard
● Overseas tourist offices: Australia Level 11, AWA Building, 47 York Street, Sydney, NSW 2000 ☎ 02 9290 2882/8; fax 02 9290 2555
UK ✉ Carrington House, 126–30 Regent Street, London W1B 5JX ☎ 020 7437 0033; fax 020 7734 2191
US ✉ 1156 Avenue of the Americas, Suite 702, New York, NY 10036 ☎ 212/302 4861; fax 212/302 4801 and ✉ 4929 Wilshire Boulevard, Suite 510, Beverly Hills, CA 90010 ☎ 323/677 0808; fax 323 677 0801

BUSES

● Buses take exact change, though you can always give a dollar coin for a journey you know costs less.
● Buses are numerous and frequent. Buy individual tickets on the bus (exact change only), or use the ez-link card.
● Machines at the front of the bus take the card; press a button for the price of your particular journey. If you're not sure of the amount, ask the driver.
● A comprehensive bus and MRT timetable, called the Transitlink Guide, can be purchased at newsagents for S$1.50.
● Singapore Bus Service runs a hotline ⊕ Mon–Fri 8–5.30, Sat 8–1. Tell them where you are and where you want to go. The number is ☎ 1800 767 4333.
● SMRT Buses also operate a night service, called the NightRider, offering late or early morning travelers a safe and affordable means of travel. The fare for this service is S$3 per trip regardless of whether you are paying by cash or ez-link card. Concessionary travel is not available for this service.

MRT

● There are three main mass rapid transit (MRT) lines; north–south, east–west and north–east.
● Trains run between 5.30am and 12.30am.
● You can buy single tickets, or use the S$7 tourist souvenir stored-value cards for a number of journeys.
● The ez-link card, also a stored-value card (minimum value S$10 plus S$5 deposit), can be used on buses as well as the MRT.
● Tickets can be purchased from machines and from ticket offices. Insert them into machines at the barriers when entering and leaving stations. Take the card with you when you are through the barrier, unless it is a single-journey ticket, in which case the machine will retain the ticket at the end of your journey.

● At the end of your stay refunds can be obtained on any amount outstanding on stored-value cards.
● Useful numbers:
● MRT ☎ 1800 767 4333; MRT and bus integration ☎ 1800 336 8900

TAXIS

● Taxis are easily found on Singapore's roads, though they can be more difficult to come by during rush hours (8am–9am and 5pm–7pm), just before midnight, and when it's raining.
● Shopping centers, hotels, sights and stations usually have taxi stands, and apart from these, taxis can also be hailed along the road. A taxi displaying a light at night is for hire.
● Taxis are air-conditioned and comfortable.
● Taxis charge a surcharge of S$2.50. There are surcharges for taxis hired from the airport, for fares between midnight and 6am, for bookings made in advance, for rush hours and for journeys via the business district or on roads where electronic road-pricing schemes are operating.
● Taxi drivers sometimes may not have sufficient change to accept large notes (S$50 or higher), so carry some low-value notes.
● Reserve in advance for important journeys, such as to the airport. Some taxi companies:
Comfort ☎ 6552 1111
Citycab ☎ 6552 2222
Comfort Premier Cabs ☎ 6552 2828

TRISHAWS

● Singapore's trishaws are now confined to a few inner-city locations where they can be hired for a ride back in time. Tour operators will also organize group tours to the back streets of Chinatown and Little India. Trishaw rides last an average of 30–45 minutes and cost from S$25 per person.
● Tour around Chinatown: Singapore Explorer ☎ 6339 6833. Trishaw tour starts from Chinatown Trishaw Park.

NEIGHBORHOODS

● Singapore's near-city neighborhoods—each one with a distinct character—are within easy reach by bus or MRT (Mass Rapid Transit). South of the river, Chinatown comes alive at festival time and just to the north is the CBD, with its tall office towers; across the river, the colonial district is set around the Padang, several museums and Raffles Hotel. Heading westward, busy Orchard Road is an international retail hub and along Serangoon Road, to the north, Indian culture thrives. Nearby Kampung Glam has long been at the heart of Malay culture. But try to discover some more out-of-the-way places, such as delightful Pulau Ubin, on the northeast of the island, or any one of the masses of public housing precincts where Singaporeans live.

VISITORS WITH DISABILITIES

Many hotels, shops and sights have facilities for people with disabilities, though getting around can sometimes be difficult because the MRT and buses are not wheelchair friendly.
If you have specific queries about particular problems, contact the National Council of Social Services ☎ 6336 1544.

Essential Facts

Check your insurance policy and purchase supplementary cover if necessary. Make sure you are covered for medical expenses.

MONEY

The unit of currency is the Singapore dollar. Brunei dollar notes have the same value as the Singapore dollar and are accepted everywhere in Singapore. The Singapore dollar and other major currencies are easily changed to local currency in Malaysia and Indonesia. Traveler's checks are readily accepted.

10 dollars

50 dollars

100 dollars

1000 dollars

MAGAZINES AND NEWSPAPERS

● The main English-language dailies are the *Straits Times*, the *Business Times* and the *New Paper*. The latter is of a tabloid nature, seen as a fun alternative to others and as a result contains very little real news.

● The *International Herald Tribune* is also available, as is a wide range of local and international magazines and publications.

MAIL

● Post office hours vary, but the post office at 1 Killiney Road is open Mon–Sat 9–9, Sun 9–4.30.

● Buy stamps in small shops and hotel lobbies, as well as at post offices.

● Postcards and airmail letters to all destinations cost 50 cents. Standard letter rate to Europe/US is S$1. Prepaid postcards and airmail letters are available.

MEDICAL TREATMENT

● Singapore's medical system is world-class. It offers a mixture of public and private treatment options. Make sure you have insurance cover.

● Many hotels offer guests a doctor-on-call service or can recommend a local doctor or clinic for you.

● If you require hospital treatment, you will need to provide proof that you can pay for it.

● The best centrally located hospitals are Mount Elizabeth (☎ 6737 2666) and Gleneagles (☎ 6473 7222). Both have emergency departments.

● Most medicines are available in Singapore.

MONEY MATTERS

● You can change money at the airport on arrival, or at hotels, banks and money-changers, who can be found all over town (and whose rate is slightly better than that given by banks and hotels). Most major banks are in the Central Business District (CBD).

● ATMs are everywhere.

● Many shops, restaurants and hotels take credit cards.

OPENING HOURS
● Stores: usually Mon–Sat 10–9.30; some close earlier and others keep longer hours. Most shops are open on Sunday.
● Banks: Mon–Fri 9–3, Sat 10–12.
● Offices: usually Mon–Fri 9–5; some open for half a day on Saturday and others open earlier and close later.
● Doctors' clinics: Mon–Fri 9–6, Sat 9–noon.

PUBLIC HOLIDAYS
● New Year's Day: 1 January
● Hari Raya Puasa: one day, January/February
● Chinese New Year: two days, January/February
● Good Friday: March/April
● Hari Raya Haji: one day, April
● Labour Day: 1 May
● Vesak Day: one day, May
● National Day: 9 August
● Diwali: November
● Christmas Day: 25 December

TELEPHONES
● Phone calls within Singapore are very cheap—local calls cost as little as 10 cents for three-minute blocks.
● Both coin- and card-operated telephones are easy to find. Most restaurants and coffee shops, as well as most shops and sights, have public phones. Phones can also be found at MRT stations.
● Phone cards can be purchased at stores and post offices.
● Calls from some hotels are subject to a 20 percent surcharge.
● International calls need to be prefixed by 001, followed by the country code. To call Singapore from outside, use country code 65.
● Operator to call for Singapore numbers ☎ 100; international numbers ☎ 104

EMBASSIES AND CONSULATES
● Australia ✉ 25 Napier Road ☎ 6836 4100 🕓 Mon–Fri 8.30–12.30 and 1.30–5
● Canada ✉ 80 Anson Road, 14–00 IBM Towers ☎ 6325 3200 🕓 Mon–Fri 8.30–11.30
● India ✉ 31 Grange Road ☎ 6737 6777 🕓 Mon–Fri 9–5.30
● Indonesia ✉ 7 Chatsworth Road ☎ 6737 7422 🕓 Mon–Fri 8.30–5
● Ireland ✉ 541 Orchard Road, 08–00 Liat Towers ☎ 6238 7616 🕓 9.30–12.30, 2–4.30
● Malaysia ✉ 301 Jervois Road ☎ 6235 0111 🕓 Mon–Fri 8–4.15
● New Zealand ✉ 391A Orchard Road, 15–06 Ngee Ann City Tower A ☎ 6235 9966 🕓 Mon–Fri 9.30–4
● UK ✉ 100 Tanglin Road ☎ 6424 4200 🕓 Mon–Fri 8.30–5
● US ✉ 27 Napier Road ☎ 6476 9100 🕓 Mon–Fri 8.30–3.30

LOST PROPERTY
● Police ☎ 999
● For lost credit cards: American Express ☎ 1800 737 8188;
Diners Card ☎ 6294 4222;
MasterCard ☎ 1800 110 0113;
VISA ☎ 1800 110 0344

Language

Singapore has four official languages: English, Mandarin, Malay and Tamil. English is widely understood and spoken. A patois know as Singlish is often used. Nominally English, it uses words from other languages, primarily Malay. Its clipped phrases and stresses make interesting listening. Road signs, bus destinations and tickets all appear in English, and staff in stores, hotels and places of interest speak English.

USEFUL WORDS AND PHRASES

MALAY	ENGLISH
selamat pagi	good morning
selamat petang	good afternoon
selamat malam	goodnight
selamat tinggal, selamat jalan	good-bye
api khabar?	how are you?
khabar baik	I'm fine
ya	yes
tidak	no
tidak apa	never mind
terimah kasih	thank you
sama sama	you're welcome
baiklah	OK
bila?	when?
esok	tomorrow
hari ini	today
semalam	yesterday
berapa har ganya?	how much?
mahal	expensive
murah	cheap
berapa jauh?	how far?
di mana?	where?

NUMBERS

satu	1
dua	2
tiga	3
empat	4
lima	5
sitta	6
tujuh	7
lapan	8
sembilan	9
sepuluh	10
sebelas	11
dua belas	12
tifa belas	13
dua puluh	20
tiga puluh	30
empat puluh	40
lima puluh	50
seratus	100
seribu	1,000

FOOD AND DRINK

daging lembu	beef
ayam	chicken
ikan	fish
daging babi	pork
nasi	rice
nasi goreng	fried rice
mee goreng	fried noodles
sayur	vegetables
kopi	coffee
teh	tea

DAYS

senin, isnin	Monday
selasa	Tuesday
rabu	Wednesday
khamis	Thursday
jumaat	Friday
sabtu	Saturday
ahad	Sunday

Timeline

EARLY DAYS

The first mention of Singapore comes in Chinese seafaring records of the 3rd century AD, where it is referred to as "Pu lou Chung" (island at the end of the peninsula). In the late 13th century Marco Polo noted a thriving city, possibly a satellite of the flourishing Sumatran Srivijayan empire. It could have been Singapore, then called Temasek. Sejarah Melayu (Malay annals of the 16th century) note a 13th-century Singapura (Lion City). In the late 14th century, the island's ruler, Parameswara, fled to Melaka. For 400 years Singapore was all but abandoned except for visiting pirates and fishermen.

1819 British official Thomas Stamford Raffles selects Singapore as a trading post between China and India. It is also near to newly acquired British colonies.

1826 With Penang and Melaka, Singapore becomes part of the British-run Straits Settlements.

1867 Singapore is designated a Crown Colony under British rule. It becomes a hub of international trade.

1870s Thousands of immigrants from south China begin arriving in Singapore. They work in shipyards and rubber plantations, and as small traders.

1887 Henry Ridley, director of the Botanic Gardens, propagates Asia's first rubber trees. Raffles Hotel opens.

1921 Japan's increasing military might causes the British to start building coastal defenses.

1942 Singapore falls to the Japanese.

1945 British Lord Louis Mountbatten accepts the Japanese surrender.

1954 Singapore's first elections: a legislative council is elected to advise the governor. Lee Kuan Yew helps found the People's Action Party (PAP).

Left to right: Sir Stamford Raffles, founder of Singapore; Raffles Hotel; plaque at Old Ford Factory; Chinatown temple detail; an old newspaper at Old Ford Factory; artwork at a Chinatown temple

1955 A Legislative Assembly is set up. David Marshall becomes Singapore's first chief minister.

1957 Malaya becomes independent. Singapore is a separate colony.

1959 PAP forms Singapore's first government. Lee Kuan Yew is appointed prime minister.

1963 Singapore forms the Federation of Malaysia with Malaya, Sarawak and North Borneo.

1965 Singapore leaves the Federation and becomes an independent republic.

1966 The Singapore dollar becomes the official currency.

1968 The British announce military withdrawal.

1977 2,913 acres (1,179ha) of land is reclaimed from the sea.

1990 Lee Kuan Yew steps aside, into the newly created post of senior minister.

2000 Singapore recovers from the Asian economic crisis.

2007 30th anniversary of the Singapore Arts Festival.

JAPANESE OCCUPATION

In 1942 the Japanese launched their attack on Singapore. Despite being outnumbered three to one, they gained control of the colony in just a few days, during which time tens of thousands of British, Indian and Australian troops were killed or wounded. During the occupation up to 50,000 Chinese men were executed and the Allied troops were interned or dispatched to work on the infamous "Death" railway.

LEE KUAN YEW

Lee Kuan Yew is credited with transforming Singapore from a Third World trading port to a highly developed nation. Known for hard work and discipline, he encouraged developments in housing, education, infrastructure and manufacture, with amazing results.

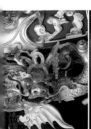

Index

A

accommodation 17, 107–112
air-conditioning 4, 10
airport 116
airport hotel 108, 117
amusement parks
 Haw Par Villa 72–73
 Sentosa 17, 62–63
antiques 11, 12, 77, 90
Arab Street 38
Asian Civilisations Museum 8, 24–25
ATMs 120

B

banks 120, 121
bars and clubs 13, 17, 18, 48–49, 91
beaches 84–85
Big Splash water rides 84
Bintan 102
Bishan HDB Estate 86
bookshops 77
Botanic Gardens 8, 56–57
Buddha Tooth Relic Temple 8, 26
budget travel 17, 109
Bugis Street 41
Bukit Timah Nature Reserve 66
buses
 long-distance 116–117
 Singapore 118

C

cableskiing 85
car rental 116
carpet auctions 77
Changi Chapel and Museum 8, 82
Chek Jawa 97
Chettiar's Temple 41
children's activities 17
Chinatown 9, 17, 28–29, 119
Chinese Garden 70
the city 20–52
 entertainment and nightlife 48–49
 map 22–23
 restaurants 50–52
 shopping 46–47
 sights 24–44
 walk 45
Clarke Quay 9, 27
classical music venues 30, 48
climate and seasons 114
coffee shops 78
colonial residences 72
credit cards 121
cricket 43
cruise ships 117
cybercafés 115

D

Da Ba Gong 100
dance, Indian 91

dehydration 101
department stores 10, 12, 36, 46, 47
Desaru 98
disabilities, visitors with 119
doctors 120, 121

E

East Coast Park 9, 84–85, 88
East Coast Sailing Centre 84
east island 79–92
 entertainment and nightlife 91
 map 80–81
 restaurants 92
 shopping 90
 sights 82–87
 walk 88
eating out 14–15, 16
 coffee 14
 hands or cutlery 14
 hawker food stands 15, 16, 106
 popiah (pancakes) 52
 satay 51
 "steamboat" 92
 see also restaurants
electrical and electronic goods 10, 12, 16, 46, 47, 90
embassies and consulates 121
entertainment and nightlife 13, 17
 the city 48–49
 east island 91
 listings 48
Esplanade 9, 30
excursions 102–103

F

fabrics 41, 90
fashion shopping 16, 47
ferries 117
festivals and events 114
fines 5
foreign exchange 120
Fuk Tak Ch'i Museum 29, 45

G

gardens
 Botanic Gardens 8, 56–57
 Chinese Garden 70
 Japanese Gardens 70
 Mandai Orchid Gardens 73
 National Orchid Garden 56–57
golf 84

H

Harbourfront 72
Haw Par Villa 72–73
health 117, 120
history 124–125
hong bao 46

hospitals 120
hostels 109
hotels 108, 109–112

I

insurance 120

J

jade 77
Japanese Gardens 70
jewelry and watches 12, 46, 90
Johor Art Gallery 103
Johor Bahru 103
Joo Chiat Road 9, 83
Jurong BirdPark 9, 18, 58–59

K

Kampung Glam 9, 31, 119
Kramat Kusu 100
Kranji War Memorial 73
Kusu Island 5, 100

L

language 122
Lau Pa Sat 9, 32
Lazarus Island 101
Little India 9, 34–35
lost property 121
Lotus Pond Temple 97

M

MacRitchie Reservoir Park 66–67
mail 120
Malay Village 86
Mandai Orchid Gardens 73–74
Marina Cove 85
Maritime Museum 62–63
markets 11, 32, 41, 47, 86, 90–91
medical treatment 120
Memories at Old Ford Factory 74–75
Mint Museum of Toys 42
money 120
mosques
 Sultan Abu Bakar Mosque 103
 Sultan Mosque 31
MRT (mass rapid transit) 118–119
museums and galleries
 Asian Civilisations Museum 8, 24–25
 Changi Chapel and Museum 8, 82
 Fuk Tak Ch'i Museum 29, 45
 Johor Art Gallery 103
 Maritime Museum 62–63
 Memories at Old Ford Factory 74–75
 Mint Museum of Toys 42
 Museum of Shanghai Toys 42

National Musuem of
  Singapore 9, 33
NUS Centre for the Arts 75
Raffles Museum 38
red dot museum 44
Republic of Singapore Air
  Force Musuem 87
Royal Sultan Abu Bakar
  Museum 103
Singapore Art Museum 8,
  39
Singapore Discovery
  Centre 8, 64–65
Singapore Science Centre
  8, 17, 68–69

N
National Musuem of
  Singapore 9, 33
National Orchid Garden 56–57
nature reserves 8, 18, 66–67,
  86–87
neighborhoods 119
netball 91
newspapers and magazines
  120
Ngee Ann City 37
night market 38
Night Safari 9, 18, 60–61
NUS Centre for the Arts 75

O
office hours 121
Omni Theater 69
opening hours 121
Orchard Road 9, 10, 36–37,
  119

P
Padang 43, 119
Pasir Ris Park 86–87
passports and visas 117
Peranakan Musuem 43
Phor Kark See 86
Planetarium 69
population 4
postal service 120
public holidays 121
public transport 118–119
Pulau Penyengat 102
Pulau Seking 98
Pulau Ubin 9, 96–97, 119
Pulau Ubin Sensory Trail 104

R
Raffles Hotel 9, 38
Raffles Museum 38
red dot museum 44
religions 4
Republic of Singapore Air
  Force Musuem 87
restaurants 14–15
  the city 50–52
  east island 92
  Singapore environs 106

west island 78
rock climbing wall 91
Royal Sultan Abu Bakar
  Museum 103

S
sailing 85
St. John's Island 5, 98
scuba diving 100–101
Sentosa 8, 17, 62–63
shophouses 28
shopping 10–12, 16, 36–37
  bargaining 47
  the city 46–47
  consumer protection 11
  east island 90
  Great Singapore Sale 114
  opening hours 121
  Singapore environs 106
  west island 73
shopping malls 12, 29, 33,
  46, 47, 77
Singapore Art Museum 8, 39
Singapore Discovery Centre
  8, 64–65
Singapore Flyer 8, 40
Singapore environs 93–106
  excursions 102–103
  map 94–95
  restaurants 106
  shopping 106
  sights 96–99
Singapore Nature Reserve 8,
  66–67
Singapore Science Centre 8,
  17, 68–69
Singapore Zoo 8, 70–71
Singlish 4
Siong Lim Temple 87
Sisters' Island 101
Sri Mariamman Temple 44
Sri Srinivasa Perumal Temple
  35
Sri Veeramakaliamman
  Temple 35
Sultan Abu Bakar Mosque
  103
Sultan Mosque 31
Sungei Buloh Wetland
  Reserve 18, 67

T
Tanjung Pinang 102
taxis 119
telephones 121
temples
  Central Sikh Temple 86
  Chettiar's Temple 41
  Da Ba Gong 100
  Lotus Pond Temple 97
  Phor Kark See 86
  Siong Lim Temple 87
  Sri Mariamman Temple 44
  Sri Srinivasa Perumal
    Temple 35

Sri Veeramakaliamman
  Temple 35
Thian Hock Keng Temple
  29
tennis 84
theater 48, 91
Thian Hock Keng Temple 29
Tiger Balm Gardens 70–71
time differences 114
tourist information 115, 118
train services 117
traveler's checks 120
travelling to Singapore 116–117
trishaws 119
turtle sanctuary 5
two-day itinerary 6–7

V
vaccinations 117

W
walks
  the city 45
  East Coast Park 88
  National Orchid Garden 56–57
  Pulau Ubin Sensory Trail
    104
websites 115
west island 53–78
  map 54–55
  restaurants 78
  shopping 77
  sights 56–75
  walk 76
wildlife 18, 58–59, 60–61, 62–
  63, 66–67, 86–87, 97

Y
YMCA 17, 109

Z
zoos
  Night Safari 9, 18, 60–61
  Singapore Zoo 8, 70–71

Singapore's
25 Best

WRITTEN BY Vivien Lytton
ADDITIONAL WRITING Rod Ritchie
UPDATED BY Graham Bond
DESIGN WORK Jacqueline Bailey
COVER DESIGN Tigist Getachew
INDEXER Marie Lorimer
IMAGE RETOUCHING AND REPRO Michael Moody and Sarah Montgomery
EDITOR Bookwork Creative Associates
REVIEWING EDITOR Linda Cabasin
SERIES EDITOR Marie-Claire Jefferies

Fodor's is a registered trademark of Random House, Inc.
Published in the United Kingdom by AA Publishing

ISBN 978-1-4000-0384-6

FOURTH EDITION

IMPORTANT TIP
Time inevitably brings changes, so always confirm prices, travel facts, and other perishable information when it matters. Although Fodor's cannot accept responsibility for errors, you can use this guide in the confidence that we have taken every care to ensure its accuracy.

SPECIAL SALES
This book is available for special discounts for bulk purchases for sales promotions or premiums. Special editions, including personalized covers, excerpts of existing books, and corporate imprints, can be created in large quantities for special needs. For more information, write to Special Markets/Premium Sales, 1745 Broadway, MD 6–2, New York, NY 10019 or email specialmarkets@randomhouse.com.

Color separation by Keenes, Andover, UK
Printed and bound by Leo Paper Products, China
10 9 8 7 6 5 4 3 2

A04461
Maps in this title produced from mapping © MAIRDUMONT / Falk Verlag 2010 and map data supplied by Global Mapping, Brackley, UK. © Global Mapping Transport map © Communicarta Ltd, UK

The Automobile Association would like to thank the following photographers, companies and picture libraries for their assistance in the preparation of this book.

Abbreviations for the picture credits are as follows: - (t) top; (b) bottom; (l) left; (r) right; (c) center; (AA) AA World Travel Library.

1 AA/N Setchfield; 2-18 Singapore Tourism Board; 4tl AA/N Setchfield; 5 AA/N Setchfield; 6cl AA/N Setchfield; 6c AA/N Setchfield; 6cr Singapore Tourism Board; 6bl AA/N Setchfield; 6bc Singapore Tourism Board; 6br Singapore Tourism Board; 7cl Media Bank; 7c AA/N Setchfield; 7cr Singapore Tourism Board; 7bl Singapore Tourism Board; 7br Brand X Pictures; 10tr Singapore Tourism Board; 10tcr AA/N Setchfield; 10/11c AA/N Setchfield; 10/11b AA/N Setchfield; 11tl AA/N Setchfield; 11tcl Singapore Tourism Board; 12 Singapore Tourism Board; 13 (i) Singapore Tourism Board; 13 (ii) Singapore Tourism Board; 13 (iii) AA/N Setchfield; 13 (iv) Singapore Tourism Board; 13 (v) Singapore Tourism Board; 14tr AA/N Setchfield; 14tcr AA/N Setchfield; 14cr AA/N Setchfield; 14br Singapore Tourism Board; 15b AA/N Setchfield; 16tr Singapore Tourism Board; 16cr AA/N Setchfield; 16bcr AA/N Setchfield; 16br AA/K Paterson; 17tl AA/N Setchfield; 17cl AA/A Kouprianoff; 17bcl AA/N Setchfield; 17bl AA/N Setchfield; 18tr AA/K Paterson; 18cr AA/N Setchfield; 18bcr AA/N Setchfield; 18br AA/N Setchfield; 19 (i) AA/N Setchfield; 19 (ii) Singapore Tourism Board; 19 (iii) AA/N Setchfield; 19 (iv) The Hantu Blog; 20/21 Singapore Tourism Board; 24tl AA/N Setchfield; 24tr AA/N Setchfield; 24/25c AA/N Setchfield; 25tr AA/N Setchfield; 25cl AA/N Setchfield; 25cr AA/N Setchfield; 26l Realimage/Alamy; 26r Steve Hamblin/Alamy; 27l AA/N Setchfield; 27r AA/N Setchfield; 28tl AA/N Setchfield; 28tr AA/N Setchfield; 28cr AA/N Setchfield; 29t Singapore Tourism Board; 29cr AA/N Setchfield; 29cl AA/N Setchfield; 30tl AA/N Setchfield; 30tr AA/N Setchfield; 31tl AA/N Setchfield; 31tc Singapore Tourism Board; 31tr AA/N Setchfield; 32l Singapore Tourism Board; 32r Singapore Tourism Board; 33l National Museum of Singapore; 33r National Museum of Singapore; 34/35t AA/N Setchfield; 34/35c AA/N Setchfield; 35t Singapore Tourism Board; 35cl AA/N Setchfield; 35cr AA/N Setchfield; 36l AA/N Setchfield; 36tr AA/N Setchfield; 36br AA/N Setchfield; 37t Singapore Tourism Board; 37bl AA/N Setchfield; 37br AA/N Setchfield; 38tl AA/N Setchfield; 38tc Media Bank; 38tr AA/N Setchfield; 39tl AA/N Setchfield; 39tc AA/N Setchfield; 39tr AA/N Setchfield; 40l Singapore Flyer Pte Ltd; 40r Singapore Flyer Pte Ltd; 41-44 AA/N Setchfield; 41l AA/N Setchfield; 41r AA/N Setchfield; 42l Mint Museum of Toys; 42r AA/N Setchfield; 43 Peranakan Museum; 44l red dot design museum, Singapore; 44r AA/N Setchfield; 45 AA/N Setchfield; 46 AA/N Setchfield; 47 AA/N Setchfield; 48-49 Singapore Tourism Board; 50 AA/N Setchfield; 51 AA/N Setchfield; 52 AA/N Setchfield; 53 Singapore Tourism Board; 56tl AA/N Setchfield; 56/57t AA/N Setchfield; 56/57c AA/N Setchfield; 56t AA/N Setchfield; 57cl AA/N Setchfield; 57cr AA/N Setchfield; 58tl AA/N Setchfield; 58/59t Singapore Tourism Board; 58/59c AA/N Setchfield; 59t Singapore Tourism Board; 59cl AA/N Setchfield; 59cr AA/N Setchfield; 60 Singapore Zoo & Night Safari; 61t Singapore Zoo & Night Safari; 61cl Singapore Zoo & Night Safari; 61cr Singapore Zoo & Night Safari; 62tl AA/N Setchfield; 62/63t AA/A Kouprianoff; 62cl AA/N Setchfield; 62/63c AA/N Setchfield; 63t AA/N Setchfield; 63cl AA/N Setchfield; 63cr AA/N Setchfield; 64tl AA/N Setchfield; 64tc Singapore Discovery Centre; 64tr AA/N Setchfield; 65 AA/N Setchfield; 66tl AA/N Setchfield; 66/67c AA/N Setchfield; 68tl AA/N Setchfield; 68/69t AA/N Setchfield; 68/69c AA/N Setchfield; 69t AA/N Setchfield; 69cl AA/N Setchfield; 69cr AA/N Setchfield; 70tl Singapore Zoo & Night Safari; 70-71t Singapore Zoo & Night Safari; 70/71c Singapore Tourism Board; 71tl Singapore Tourism Board; 71tr Singapore Zoo & Night Safari 72-75t AA/N Setchfield; 72bl AA/N Setchfield; 72br AA/N Setchfield; 73bl AA/N Setchfield; 73br AA/N Setchfield; 74 AA/N Setchfield; 75l AA/N Setchfield; 75r AA/N Setchfield; 76 AA/N Setchfield; 77 AA/N Setchfield; 78t Singapore Tourism Board; 79 AA/N Setchfield; 82tl Singapore Tourism Board; 82tr AA/N Setchfield; 83tl AA/N Setchfield; 83tr AA/N Setchfield; 84tl AA/N Setchfield; 84/85t AA/N Setchfield; 84/8cr AA/N Setchfield; 85t AA/N Setchfield; 85c AA/N Setchfield; 86-87t AA/N Setchfield; 86b AA/N Setchfield; 87bl AA/N Setchfield; 87br AA/N Setchfield; 88t AA/N Setchfield; 89 AA/N Setchfield; 90t AA/N Setchfield; 91t Singapore Tourism Board; 92t Singapore Tourism Board; 93 The Hantu Blog; 96tl AA/N Setchfield; 96/97 AA/N Setchfield; 96bl Singapore Tourism Board; 97 AA/N Setchfield; 98t AA/N Setchfield; 98b AA/N Setchfield; 99 AA/K Paterson; 100/101t The Hantu Blog; 100bl The Hantu Blog; 100cr The Hantu Blog; 100br The Hantu Blog; 101bl The Hantu Blog; 101br The Hantu Blog; 102t AA/S Strange; 102bl © Leonid Serebrennikov/Alamy; 102br © Leonid Serebrennikov/Alamy; 103t AA/N Setchfield; 103bl AA/N Hanna; 103bcr AA/N Setchfield; 103br AA/N Setchfield; 104t Singapore Tourism Board; 105t AA/N Setchfield; 105c Singapore Tourism Board; 106 AA/N Setchfield; 107 AA/N Setchfield; 108-112t AA/C Sawyer; 108tr Media Bank; 108tcr Media Bank; 108car AA/N Ray; 108br AA/N Setchfield; 113 Singapore Tourism Board; 114-125 Singapore Tourism Board; 120b MRI Bankers' Guide to Foreign Currency, Houston, USA; 123 AA/N Setchfield; 124bl AA/N Setchfield; 124bc AA/N Setchfield; 124br AA/N Setchfield; 125bl AA/N Setchfield; 125bc AA/N Setchfield; 125br AA/N Setchfield

Every effort has been made to trace the copyright holders, and we apologise in advance for any accidental errors. We would be happy to apply the corrections in the following edition of this publication.